This New
Book of Saints
is dedicated to

Saint Joseph

Patron
of the
Universal Church

Presented

to

_____

_____

by

_____

date

_____

The work of God's hands is clear in His Saints,
the beauty of His truth is shown in their faith.

SAINT JOSEPH

ILLUSTRATED
BOOK OF SAINTS

INSPIRING LIVES IN WORD AND PICTURE

Rev. Thomas J. Donaghy

ILLUSTRATED IN FULL COLOR

CATHOLIC BOOK PUBLISHING CORP.
New Jersey

FOREWORD

IN a small country church where I first attended Mass and received First Reconciliation and Holy Communion, I was fascinated by two rather large statues of our Blessed Mother and St. Joseph. One could easily understand that these were images of holy people. As we grew older, we came to realize that Our Lady, St. Joseph, and thousands of others live with God in heaven. In school, we learned the names and lives of some of the other Saints. Often, we were surprised at the different clothing they wore.

As we learned more and more about the Saints, we began to realize that their pictures and statues gave us a good idea of where and when they lived. We had opportunities to hear and read their stories, and, at the same time, come to know and understand that even though the Saints grew up in different countries and cultures, the way they lived and loved God and neighbor was something we could do.

Today, we have many role models like the astronauts, outstanding builders, artists, wholesome athletes, self-sacrificing public servants, learned researchers, professors, doctors, and judges, and, of course, our parents, brothers, and sisters. As we all know, adults often ask children the age-old question, "What do you want to be when you grow up?" It is a reasonable question, and we appreciate their interest in us. Sometimes it starts us thinking about our personal futures. The beauty is that no matter what we want to be, we can carry out our plans and dreams and still strive to be Saints.

During his years as Pope, our Holy Father, Pope John Paul II, has given us over four hundred additional role models in newly canonized Saints. These holy people not only carried out their choices in life but also, at the same time, lived holy and saintly lives.

This volume gives children and adults alike a number of role models. If we want to follow our chosen way of life while imitating the life of a particular Saint, we might want to recite each day the prayer provided for our chosen Saint. Or, we may be attracted to a number of ways other Saints lived holy lives. In any case, it is important to read and recall their good lives, and pray to one or several Saints each day. This book can easily help us follow the Saint or Saints we really want to imitate.

Father Thomas J. Donaghy

Nihil Obstat: Rev. James M. Cafone, M.A., S.T.D., Censor Librorum
Imprimatur: ✠ Most Rev. John J. Myers, J.C.D., D.D., Archbishop of Newark

The Nihil Obstat and Imprimatur are official declarations that a book or pamphlet is free of doctrinal or moral error. No implication is contained therein that those who have granted the Nihil Obstat and Imprimatur agree with the contents, opinions or statements expressed.

(T-735)

ISBN 978-0-89942-733-1

© 2003 by CATHOLIC BOOK PUBLISHING CORP., New Jersey

Printed in China
CPSIA   August 2016   10 9 8 7 6 5 4 3 2 1   L/P

CONTENTS

~ *Mother of God* ~

THE QUEENSHIP OF THE BLESSED VIRGIN MARY

August 22

ON October 11, 1954, His Holiness, Pope Pius XII, in his encyclical letter, *Ad Caeli Reginam*, decreed and instituted the feast of the Queenship of the Blessed Virgin Mary to be celebrated throughout the world every year. He declared that the Church has believed in Mary's Queenship from the earliest centuries and that this belief rests on Holy Scripture and tradition.

Mary is Queen of all "since she brought forth a Son, Who at the very moment that He was conceived, was, by reason of the hypostatic union of the human nature with the Word, even as man, King and Lord of all things." Further, "as Christ is our Lord and King by a special title because He redeemed us, so the Blessed Virgin (is our Lady and Queen) because of the unique way in which she has cooperated toward our redemption by giving of her own substance, by offering Him willingly for us, and by desiring, praying for, and bringing about our salvation in a singular manner."

The significance of Mary's Queenship for contemporary times is that her participation in the work of her Son rouses hope and expresses a merciful and furthering love. In looking to Mary as a necessary reference point, the faithful can find in her the secret to their own royal identity as children of God and the model for giving the Lord a greater place in their lives.

PRAYER: *Hail, holy Queen, Mother of mercy;*
hail, our life, our sweetness and our hope.
To you do we cry,
poor banished children of Eve.
To you do we send up our sighs,
mourning and weeping in this valley of tears.
Turn then, most gracious Advocate,
your eyes of mercy toward us.
And after this our exile
show unto us the blessed fruit of your womb,
 Jesus.
O clement, O loving, O sweet Virgin Mary.

SAINT AGNES

Virgin and Martyr

January 21

ST. AGNES suffered martyrdom at the age of thirteen, during the bloody persecution of the Emperor Diocletian around 304 and became one of the best known and most highly regarded of the Roman martyrs. Her name is still retained in the First Eucharistic Prayer for Holy Mass.

The Acts of her Passion, which date back only to the 5th century, are considered to be not entirely reliable but they do tell us something about her. The young noblemen of Rome, attracted by her wealth and beauty, vied with one another in endeavoring to obtain her hand in marriage, but she refused them all, saying that she had chosen a Spouse who could not be seen with mortal eyes. Her suitors, in hope of shaking her constancy, accused her of being a Christian.

She was brought before a judge and remained unswayed by either his kindness or his threats. Fires were kindled, instruments of torture were placed before her eyes, but, immovable in her constancy, she surveyed them with heroic calmness. She was sent to a house of prostitution, but the sight of her inspired such awe that not one of the wicked youths of the city dared approach her. One, bolder than the others, was suddenly struck with blindness and he fell trembling.

The youthful Saint came forth from this den of infamy uncontaminated in mind and body, and still a pure spouse of Christ. Her most prominent suitor was so enraged that he incited the judge still more against her. The heroic Virgin was condemned to be beheaded. "She went to the place of execution," says St. Ambrose, "more cheerfully than others go to their wedding."

Amid the tears of the spectators the instrument of death fell, and she went to meet the Immortal Spouse whom she had loved better than her life. She was buried on the Via Nomentana, and Constantine erected a church in her honor.

PRAYER: *All-powerful and ever-living God, You choose the weak in this world to confound the powerful. As we celebrate the anniversary of the martyrdom of St. Agnes, may we like her remain constant in faith.*

~ Patroness of the Children of Mary ~

~ *Patron of Catholic Youth* ~

SAINT ALOYSIUS GONZAGA

Religious

June 21

THIS youthful scion of the illustrious house of Gonzaga, son of Ferdinand, Marquis of Castiglione, was born at Castiglione in the diocese of Brescia, March 9, 1568. From his tenderest years St. Aloysius devoted himself heart and soul to the service of his Creator. His memory has come to us with the sweet fragrance of the most unsullied purity. He united an innocence perfectly angelic with a penance truly heroic.

At fourteen years of age he accompanied his father to Spain, where the latter went to attend the Empress, Maria of Austria, wife of Maximilian II. Philip II made him page to Prince James, elder brother of Philip II. His innocence remained uncontaminated amid the vanities of the court, nor could the world draw his heart from God.

On his return to Italy in 1584, he manifested his desire to enter the Society of Jesus. In spite of opposition, he finally succeeded in carrying out his intentions and became a novice at Rome in 1585, during the pontificate of Pope Pius V. He made his profession November 20, 1587, and soon after received minor orders.

From the beginning of his religious life St. Aloysius was a model of perfection. Jesuit Robert Bellarmine exerted influence on Aloysius in his later years, guiding the development of his courageous and single-minded devotion to God.

During an epidemic in Rome in 1591, he distinguished himself by his charity toward the sick in the hospital. These labors brought on him the illness that ended in his death. His last days were the faithful echo of his briefly consummated life. He exchanged time for eternity on June 21, 1591, at twenty-four years of age. St. Aloysius was canonized in 1726 by Pope Benedict XIII and declared patron of Catholic youth in 1729.

PRAYER: *God, Author of all heavenly gifts, You gave St. Aloysius both a wonderful innocence of life and a deep spirit of penance. Through his merits grant that we may imitate his penitence.*

— 15 —

SAINT ALPHONSUS LIGUORI

Bishop and Doctor of the Church

August 1

ST. ALPHONSUS was born in the village of Marianella near Naples, Italy, September 27, 1696. At a tender age his pious mother inspired him with the deepest sentiments of piety. The education he received under the auspices of his father, aided by his own intellect, produced in him such results that at the early age of sixteen he graduated in law. Shortly after, he was admitted to the Neapolitan bar. In 1723, he lost a case, and God made use of his disappointment to wean his heart from the world. In spite of all opposition he now entered the ecclesiastical state.

In 1726, he was ordained a priest. He exercised the ministry at various places with great fruit, zealously laboring for his own sanctification.

In 1732, God called him to found the Congregation of the Most Holy Redeemer, with the object of laboring for the salvation of the most abandoned souls. Amid untold difficulties and innumerable trials, St. Alphonsus succeeded in establishing his Congregation, which became his glory and crown, but also his cross. The holy founder labored incessantly at the work of the missions until, about 1756, he was appointed Bishop of St. Agatha, a diocese he governed until 1775, when, broken by age and infirmity, he resigned this office to retire to his monastery where he died.

Few Saints have labored as much, either by word or by writing, as St. Alphonsus. He was a prolific and popular author, the utility of whose works will never cease. His last years were characterized by intense suffering, which he bore with resignation. His happy death occurred at Nocera de Pagani, August 1, 1787. He was canonized in 1839 by Pope Gregory XVI and declared Doctor of the Church in 1871 by Pope Pius IX.

PRAYER: *God, You constantly introduce new examples of virtue in Your Church. Walking in the footsteps of St. Alphonsus Your Bishop, may we be consumed with zeal for souls and attain the rewards he has won in heaven.*

~ Patron of Confessors and Theologians ~

~ Patron of Candlemakers ~

SAINT AMBROSE

Bishop and Doctor of the Church

December 7

ST. AMBROSE was born in Gaul, where his father exercised the office of Prefect of the Praetorium, about the year 340. His father died while he was still an infant, and with his mother he returned to Rome, where he enjoyed a good education, learned the Greek language, and became a good poet and orator. Later he moved to Milan with his brother.

Probus, Praetorian Prefect of Italy, appointed Ambrose Governor of Liguria and Aemilia. His virtues in this office, and the voice of a child who proclaimed him Bishop, marked him out to the people of Milan as their Bishop on the vacancy of the See. Both Catholics and Arians elected him to the first dignity in the diocese, a dignity that he reluctantly accepted. As he was only a catechumen, he received the Sacrament of Baptism, after which he was consecrated Bishop, in 374, at the age of thirty-four.

After giving his fortune to the Church and the poor, he applied himself to study the Scriptures and ecclesiastical writers, placing himself under the instruction of Simplicianus, a priest of the Church of Rome, who succeeded him in the Archbishopric of Milan. His warfare against the Arians was such that by the year 385 very few still professed that heresy in the diocese. In 381, he held a Council at Milan against the heresy of Apollinaris, and assisted at that of Aquileia; the next year, he assisted at one held in Rome.

When Maximus assumed the purple in Gaul, St. Ambrose was sent there, and he succeeded in concluding a treaty with the Emperor. But a second embassy, in 387, was not so successful: Maximus invaded Italy and was defeated by the Emperor Theodosius. St. Ambrose at a later date had occasion to reprehend Theodosius and did so with the greatest apostolical freedom.

He witnessed the conversion of the great St. Augustine, whom he baptized in 387. One of his last actions was the ordination of St. Honoratus. After a life of labor and prayer the holy Bishop of Milan died in 397.

PRAYER: *God, by Your grace St. Ambrose, Your Bishop, became a great teacher of the Catholic Faith. Raise up Bishops in Your Church today who will give strong and wise leadership.*

SAINT ANDREW

Apostle

November 30

ST. ANDREW, the brother of St. Peter, was a native of the town of Bethsaida in Galilee, and a fisherman by profession. Being first a disciple of St. John the Baptist, whose apostolate was one of conversion to prepare people for the coming Messiah, he later joined Jesus, and also brought to Him his brother, with whom he became a member of the Apostolic College.

Besides his inclusion in the listing of the Apostles, Andrew is also mentioned in Scripture in two incidents along with Philip the Apostle. The first of these incidents is the multiplication of the loaves and fish as reported in the sixth chapter of the Gospel of John. Andrew reports to Jesus, "There is a lad here who has five barley loaves and a couple of dried fish, but what good is that for so many?"

In the other episode, later in the Gospel of John, a group of Greeks had asked Philip to introduce them to Jesus, and Andrew served along with Philip as their intermediary.

After the dispersion of the Apostles, St. Andrew preached the Gospel in Scythia, as we learn from Origen; and, as Sophronius says, also in Sogdiana and Colchis. According to Theodoret, St. Gregory Nazianzen, and St. Jerome, he also labored in Greece. It is even believed that he carried the Gospel as far as Russia and Poland, and that he preached at Byzantium. He suffered martyrdom at Patras in Achaia, and, according to ancient authorities, by crucifixion on a cross in the form of an X.

The body of the Saint was taken to Constantinople in 357, and deposited in the Church of the Apostles, built by Constantine the Great. In 1270, when the city fell into the hands of the Latins, the relics were transported to Italy and deposited in the Cathedral of Amalfi.

PRAYER: *Lord, You raised up St. Andrew, Your Apostle, to preach and rule in Your Church. Grant that we may always experience the benefit of his intercession with You.*

~ *Patron of Fishermen* ~

~ Foundress of the Ursulines ~

SAINT ANGELA MERICI

Virgin

January 27

BORN in 1474 at Desenzano on the shore of Lake Garda, Italy, St. Angela Merici became a tertiary of St. Francis at fifteen. In a vision God revealed to her that she would establish a "company" to promote the welfare of souls. At Desenzano she established a school for the instruction of young girls and a second school at Brescia. She gathered around her twelve religious companions and founded the Ursulines at Brescia.

St. Angela was of a reflective bent and possibly the first to grasp the changed role of women in the society transformed by the Renaissance. She envisaged that those who joined her would remain in the world but devote themselves to every type of corporal and spiritual work of mercy, with special emphasis on education.

However, her idea of education was very different from that of a convent school. She preferred to send her followers to teach girls in their own families. Through this she hoped to effect an improvement in social conditions. For it was her belief that "disorder in society is the result of disorder in the family." Her idea of a religious order of women without distinctive habit and without solemn vows and enclosure was also in advance of her times—although her Order was obliged to adopt the canonical safeguards then required of all nuns.

On November 25, 1535, the solemn canonical institution of the company of St. Ursula took place in the Oratory of the Piazza del Duomo. As a patron, St. Angela chose St. Ursula because ever since her martyrdom, St. Ursula was regarded as the ideal type of Christian virginity.

The schools of the Ursulines did their share in strengthening and extending Catholicism and in safeguarding Italy from what we now term "modern unbelief." She was canonized in 1807 by Pope Pius VII.

PRAYER: *Lord, let St. Angela never cease commending us to Your kindness. By always imitating her charity and prudence may we succeed in keeping Your teachings and preserving good morals.*

SAINT ANNE

Mother of Mary

July 26

ST. ANNE, of the tribe of Judah of the royal house of David, is venerated by the Church as the mother of the Blessed Virgin Mary and the grandmother of Jesus.

She and her husband, St. Joachim, acted with great devotion to God in their everyday life in Nazareth. Yet, when they had no children, it was believed by those around them that God was punishing them.

Their prayers for a child were finally answered, even though Anne was considered to be too old to have children. They called the daughter born to them Miriam or "Mary." The other Mary mentioned in the Gospels as the sister of the Mother of God was, it is believed, her cousin, for this was a customary way of designating relatives in the East. St. Anne offered Mary, Jesus' Mother, to the service of God at a very early age.

St. Anne has been honored from early Christian times. Churches were dedicated to her honor, and the Fathers, especially of the Eastern Churches, loved to speak of her sanctity and privileges. She is often represented as teaching her little daughter to read the Scriptures.

St. Anne's name means "grace." God gave her special graces, and the greatest was that she was the mother of the Mother of God. It is no wonder that St. Anne is the patron of mothers and of children.

Tradition, grounded on very old testimonies, informs us that Sts. Joachim and Anne in their old age came from Galilee to settle in Jerusalem, and there the Blessed Mother of God was born and reared; there also they died and were buried. A church was built during the fourth century, possibly by St. Helena, on the site of the home of Sts. Joachim and Anne in Jerusalem.

PRAYER: *Lord, God of our fathers, through St. Anne You gave us the Mother of Your Incarnate Son. May her prayers help us to attain the salvation You promised to Your people.*

~ *Patroness of Christian Mothers* ~

— 25 —

~ *Founder of the Claretians* ~

SAINT ANTHONY MARY CLARET

Bishop

October 24

BORN in Sallent, Spain, in 1807, the son of a weaver, St. Anthony was ordained a priest in 1835, after having entered the seminary at Vich when he was twenty-two years of age. Five years later, he began to give missions and retreats all over Catalonia and the Canary Islands. Seeing their success and the people's need for them, he founded (in 1849) the Congregation of the Missionary Sons of the Immaculate Heart of Mary (Claretians) to continue this work on a wider scale.

In that same year, he was consecrated Archbishop of Santiago de Cuba. Amid great opposition and finding the diocese in a deplorable spiritual condition, he quickly initiated vigorous reform measures, one of which was the establishment of the Teaching Sisters of Mary Immaculate.

In 1857, he was recalled to Spain by Pope Pius XI and made the chaplain of Queen Isabella II. This position made it possible for him to continue his mission work by preaching and publishing good literature. It is believed that some ten thousand sermons are attributed to St. Anthony, as well as approximately two hundred books or pamphlets that sought to instruct and edify both clerics and laypeople.

He established a museum, library, schools, and a laboratory, also helping to revive the Catalan language. He spread devotion to the Blessed Sacrament and the Immaculate Heart of Mary, and after the revolution of 1868 ended his life in exile with the Queen. He died in the Cistercian monastery of Fontfroide, near Narbonne, on October 24, 1870. He was canonized in 1950 by Pope Pius XII.

PRAYER: *God, You strengthened St. Anthony Mary with wondrous love and patience in evangelizing the people. Through his intercession, enable us to seek those things that are Yours, and to labor in Christ for the good of our fellow men.*

SAINT ANTHONY OF PADUA

Priest and Doctor of the Church

June 13

ST. ANTHONY, called "St. Anthony of Padua" on account of his long residence in that city, was a native of Lisbon in Portugal, where he was born in 1195, receiving the name of Ferdinand at his Baptism. At an early age his parents placed him in the community of the Canons of the Cathedral of Lisbon, by whom he was educated. At fifteen he entered the Order of Regular Canons of St. Augustine near Lisbon. After two years he was sent to the convent of the Holy Cross of the same Order at Coimbra.

He had lived in this house eight years, intent on his studies, when the relics of five Franciscan martyrs were brought from Morocco to Portugal. This event inspired him to follow in the footsteps of these heroes of the Faith. When this became known his brethren offered extreme opposition, but he finally obtained the consent of the prior and passed over to the Franciscan Order.

After some time he obtained leave to go to Africa to preach to the Moors, but a severe illness obliged him to return to Spain. However, the vessel was driven to Sicily by contrary winds, and the desire to see St. Francis took him to Assisi, where a general chapter of the Order was in progress. At first he was entirely ignored in the Order, and he purposely kept himself in obscurity; but Providence soon revealed to the Franciscans what a treasure they had acquired, and St. Anthony was made professor of theology.

In time, he gave up teaching to devote himself to preaching, for he was an accomplished orator. In this work he traveled through France, Spain, and Italy. He was invested with several important dignities in his Order and labored hard to preserve monastic discipline, boldly opposing the famous General Elias, who sought to introduce relaxations. He died June 13, 1231, and was canonized the following year by Pope Gregory IX.

PRAYER: *Almighty, ever-living God, You gave Your people the extraordinary preacher St. Anthony and made him an intercessor in difficulties. By his aid grant that we may live a truly Christian life and experience Your help in all adversities.*

~ Patron of the Poor ~

~ *Patron of Theologians* ~

SAINT AUGUSTINE
Bishop and Doctor of the Church
August 28

S T. AUGUSTINE was born on November 13, 354, at Tagaste (modern Algeria) in Africa. In spite of the piety of his holy mother, St. Monica, he fell at an early age into sinful ways and even at a later period became a heretic of the sect of the Manicheans. Unfortunately, his father, Patricius, was then an idolater, so that the youth met with little or no restraint. In the beginning of 370 he continued his studies at Carthage. The following year his father died, after being converted to Christianity.

Some time later, St. Augustine took up his abode at Carthage and opened a school of rhetoric. Later he went to Rome and then to Milan, where he also began to teach rhetoric. Here God's grace and the prayers of his mother, who had followed him to Italy, as well as the instructions of saintly friends, particularly of St. Ambrose, effected his conversion. He abandoned the sect of the Manicheans, and after some time gave himself entirely to God. St. Ambrose baptized him on Easter eve, 387.

On his return to Africa, the Saint lost his mother at Ostia in the same year, and in 388 he arrived at Carthage. At Tagaste he began to live a community life with some of his friends. He was ordained in 390 and moved to Hippo. Five years later he was consecrated Bishop and made coadjutor to Valerius, Bishop of Hippo, whom he succeeded in the following year.

From this period until his death his life was one of ceaseless activity. He governed his church, preached to his people, and wrote voluminous works that have received the admiration of the ages. His humility prompted him to write his *Confessions* about the year 397, and from this work we have a detailed account of his early years.

Shortly before his death the Vandals under Genseric invaded Africa, and the Saint was witness of the desolation that followed in their tracks. This multi-faceted religious genius and devout servant of God died on August 28, 430.

PRAYER: *Lord, filled by the spirit of St. Augustine, may we thirst after You as the true Source of wisdom.*

SAINT BARNABAS
Apostle

THOUGH not one of the original Twelve, St. Barnabas is considered an Apostle by the Church. He was a Jew of the tribe of Levi, but born in Cyprus, where the family settled. His success in preaching prompted the Apostles to change his name of Joseph to that of Barnabas—which means "son of exhortation" or "consolation." He also was noted for his generosity in the early Christian community of Jerusalem (Acts 4:36–37).

It was St. Barnabas who, amid the Apostles' skepticism, befriended the recently converted and former persecutor of the Church, Saul of Tarsus, and set him on the path to becoming the great Apostle Paul by introducing him to the Apostles (Acts 9:27). When St. Barnabas went to Antioch to consolidate the infant Church there, he asked St. Paul to share his labors. After laboring a year at Antioch, the two Apostles brought the offerings of the community to the famine-stricken poor of the Judean community (Acts 11:27–30).

Together with St. Paul, Barnabas preached the Faith in Cyprus and central Asia (Acts 13—14) and attended the First Council of Jerusalem (Acts 15:1–29). But on their return to Antioch they parted company when St. Barnabas wanted his nephew John Mark to accompany them on their second missionary journey while St. Paul did not (Acts 15:30–40); accordingly, St. Barnabas went back to Cyprus with John Mark (Acts 15:30–40). This rift apparently healed, for Paul spoke of Barnabas in complimentary terms in later writings.

The subsequent events of the life of St. Barnabas are not certain, except that he was known to the Corinthians (1 Cor 9:6). A tradition relates that he died at Salamis in Cyprus, after being stoned.

PRAYER: *God, you commanded that St. Barnabas, full of Faith and the Holy Spirit, should be set apart to labor for the conversion of the Gentiles. May Christ's Gospel which he preached with great ardor continue to be preached faithfully by word and deed.*

~ *Patron of Milan and Florence* ~

— 33 —

~ *Patron of Plasterers* ~

SAINT BARTHOLOMEW

Apostle

August 24

MANY Scripture scholars identify (reasonably but not conclusively) St. Bartholomew with Nathaniel who was conducted to Christ by St. Philip. The name of Bartholomew signifies son of Tolmai, and it was given to the Saint in the same sense that "Bar Jonah" was attached to St. Peter.

Although Bartholomew found it hard to believe that Jesus, the Messiah, came from the poor town of Nazareth, Jesus convinced him that He was the One Whom Bartholomew read of in the Bible. He was subsequently chosen by our Lord Himself to be one of the Twelve Apostles. This Apostle was on the lake shore when Jesus showed Himself after the Resurrection and had breakfast with some of His followers.

According to Eusebius and other ancient writers, he preached the Gospel in the most barbarous countries of the East, penetrating as far as India. Eusebius relates that when St. Pantaenus, in the third century, went to India, he still found the knowledge of Christ in that country, and a copy of the Gospel of St. Matthew in Hebrew was shown to him, which he was told had been brought there by St. Bartholomew.

St. John Chrysostom declares that St. Bartholomew brought the Faith to the people of Lycaonia. According to St. Gregory of Tours, the last field of his labors was Great Armenia, where, preaching in a place obstinately addicted to the worship of idols, he suffered martyrdom. By some it is said that he was flayed alive; by others that he suffered crucifixion—both these opinions being reconcilable. The relics of the Saint are preserved in the church of St. Bartholomew on the island in the Tiber River near Rome.

PRAYER: *Lord, strengthen in us that Faith by which Your Apostle St. Bartholomew adhered to Your Son with sincerity of mind. Through his intercession, grant that Your Church may become a sacrament of salvation for all nations.*

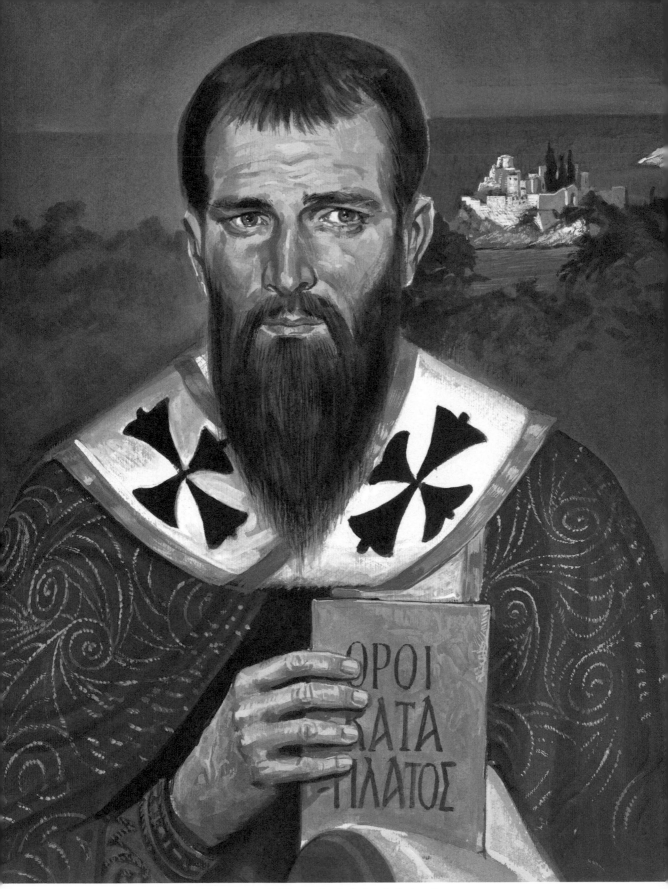

~ Patron of Hospital Administrators ~

SAINT BASIL THE GREAT

Bishop and Doctor of the Church

January 2

IN the revision of the calendar the Church has seen fit to honor Sts. Basil the Great and Gregory Nazianzen, two great Doctors of the Church and fast friends, on the same day.

St. Basil the Great was born at Caesarea of Cappadocia in 330, the son of a rhetorician from a distinguished and pious family. Both of his parents and several of his ten brothers and sisters are honored among the Saints. He attended school in Caesarea, as well as Constantinople and Athens, where he became acquainted with St. Gregory Nazianzen in 352. A little later, he opened a school of oratory in Caesarea and practiced law.

Eventually he decided to sell all his goods, give the money from the sale to the poor, and become a monk. He founded a monastery in Pontus, the first in Asia Minor, which he directed for five years.

He wrote a famous monastic rule that has proved the most enduring of those in the East.

After founding several other monasteries, he was ordained and, in 370, made Archbishop of Caesarea. In this post (until his death in 379), despite poor health, he continued to be a man of vast learning and constant activity, genuine eloquence, and immense charity.

In the midst of religious and political controversy, he made time to build a hospice and a far-reaching facility for ministering to the sick and focused his efforts to combat the moral and physical ills of society.

Basil wrote many books and was a staunch defender of the Church against the heresy of Arianism. His deeds and character earned for him the title of "Great" during his life and Doctor of the Church after his death.

PRAYER: *Lord God, You desired to enlighten Your Church by the life and teachings of St. Basil. Grant that we may learn Your truth with humility and faithfully put it into practice with love.*

SAINT BENEDICT

Abbot

July 11

THE Patriarch of Western monasticism was born of a noble family at Nursia, in central Italy, about 480. Most of what is known of his life comes from Gregory's *Dialogues*. In his youth, seeing the corruption of the world, he left home to live a hermit's life of penance and prayer in a cave in the mountain of Subiaco, some forty miles from Rome, where he was instructed in Christian asceticism by St. Romanus, a Solitary of the vicinity.

His reputation for sanctity gathered a large number of disciples around him, for whom he erected monasteries in which they lived a community life—praying, clearing the land, planting crops, teaching school, feeding the poor—under a prescribed rule. In the year 529, he left Subiaco for Monte Cassino, near the city of Naples in Italy, and there founded the great Abbey that became the center of religious life in Europe.

St. Scholastica, the sister of St. Benedict, was the first Benedictine nun. She presided over a monastery of nuns near Monte Cassino.

The principles of the Rule written by St. Benedict, whose motto was "Pray and work," became the basis of religious life for all Western religious orders and congregations after his time. It shows the way to religious perfection by the practice of self-conquest, mortification, humility, obedience, prayer, silence, prudence, moderation, stability, retirement, and detachment from the world and its cares. His monastic way of life was orderly, workable, and complete.

St. Benedict died March 21, 547, as he stood before the altar of Monte Cassino immediately after receiving Holy Communion. It is said that his monks held up his arms in prayer as he received the Blessed Sacrament.

PRAYER: *God, You established St. Benedict the Abbot as an admirable teacher in the school of Divine servitude. Teach us never to prefer anything to Your love and always to run the way of Your Commandments with most generous dispositions.*

~ Patron of Poison Sufferers ~

~ Lived a Life of Joyful Suffering ~

— 40 —

SAINT BERNADETTE

Virgin

April 16

ST. MARIE BERNADETTE SOUBIROUS was born to a poor family at Lourdes, France, in 1844. At fourteen years of age, she witnessed eighteen apparitions of Our Blessed Lady at Lourdes. In the first of these, Bernadette was gathering firewood, and a beautiful Lady, dressed in blue and white, stood before her in a cave, or grotto. She smiled at Bernadette and asked her to say the Rosary with her.

Our Lady asked Bernadette to spread important messages to the world. She wanted people to know that they must do penance for their sins and pray. The Blessed Mother also wanted Bernadette to make known the miraculous healing powers of the waters at Lourdes that Our Lady, by her very presence, made possible. When she asked Bernadette to scrape the earth there, the spring started to flow. The Blessed Virgin also revealed herself to Bernadette as the Immaculate Conception.

Large crowds followed Bernadette to the grotto to pray the Rosary with her. Many people traveled there then and have done so since to be healed by the flowing waters.

In 1866 St. Marie Bernadette Soubirous joined the Sisters of Charity at Nevers, taking her perpetual vows in 1878. Her contemporaries admired her humility and the authentic character of her testimony about the appearance of the Blessed Virgin.

Nevertheless she had to endure many severe trials during her religious life and exhibited heroic patience in sickness. She realized that the healing spring was not for her, and was fond of saying: "The Blessed Virgin used me as a broom to remove dust. When the work is finished, the broom is placed behind the door and left there." She died in 1879 at the age of thirty-five and was canonized in 1933 by Pope Pius XI.

PRAYER: *Lord God, You showered heavenly gifts on St. Bernadette. Help us to imitate her virtues during our earthly life and enjoy eternal happiness with her in heaven.*

SAINT BERNARD

Abbot and Doctor of the Church

August 20

ST. BERNARD was born of noble parentage in Burgundy, France. Under the care of his pious parents he was sent at an early age to a college at Chatillon, where he was recognized for his remarkable piety and spirit of recollection. There he entered upon the studies of theology and Holy Scripture. After the death of his mother, fearing the snares and temptations of the world, he resolved to embrace the newly established and austere institute of the Cistercian Order, of which he was destined to become the greatest ornament. He also persuaded his brothers and several of his friends to follow his example.

In 1113, St. Bernard, with thirty young noblemen, presented himself to the holy Abbot, St. Stephen, at Cîteaux. After a novitiate spent in great fervor, he made his profession in the following year. His superior soon after, seeing the great progress he had made in the spiritual life, sent him with twelve monks to found a new monastery, which afterward became known as the celebrated Abbey of Clairvaux. St. Bernard was at once appointed Abbot and began the active life that has rendered him the most conspicuous figure in the history of the twelfth century.

He founded numerous other monasteries, composed a number of works and undertook many journeys for the honor of God. Several Bishoprics were offered him, but he refused them all. His reputation spread far and wide; even the Popes were governed by his advice.

He was commissioned by Pope Eugene III to preach the second Crusade. In obedience to the Sovereign Pontiff he traveled through France and Germany, and aroused the greatest enthusiasm for the holy war among the masses of the population. The failure of the expedition raised a great storm against the Saint, but he attributed it to the sins of the Crusaders. St. Bernard was eminently endowed with the gift of miracles. He died on August 20, 1153, and was canonized in 1174 by Pope Alexander III.

PRAYER: *God, You blessed Your Church with St. Bernard, a man full of zeal for Your house, radiating brightness and ardent love. Through his intercession, grant that we may be animated by the same spirit.*

~ *Patron of the Cistercians* ~

~ Patron of the Franciscans ~

SAINT BONAVENTURE

Bishop and Doctor of the Church

July 15

ST. BONAVENTURE, widely known as "The Seraphic Doctor," was born at Bagnorea in Tuscany in 1221. Originally called John, he received the name of Bonaventure from St. Francis of Assisi, when, in response to the pleading of the child's mother, the Saint prayed for John's recovery from a dangerous illness, and, foreseeing the future greatness of the little John, cried out, "O buona ventura"—O good fortune!

At twenty-two St. Bonaventure entered the Franciscan Order. Having made his vows, he was sent to Paris to complete his studies under the celebrated doctor Alexander of Hales, an Englishman and a Franciscan. After the latter's death he continued his course under his successor, John of Rochelle. In Paris he became the intimate friend of the great St. Thomas Aquinas. He received the degree of Doctor, together with St. Thomas Aquinas, ceding to his friend, against the latter's inclination, the honor of having it first conferred upon him. Like St. Thomas, he enjoyed the friendship of the holy King, St. Louis.

At the age of thirty-five he was chosen General of his Order and restored a perfect calm where peace had been disturbed by internal dissensions. He did much for his Order and composed the life of St. Francis. He also assisted at the translation of the relics of St. Anthony of Padua. He was nominated Archbishop of York by Pope Clement IV, but he begged not to be forced to accept that dignity. Gregory X obliged him to take upon himself a greater one, that of Cardinal and Bishop of Albano, one of the six suffragan Sees of Rome. Before his death he abdicated his office of General of the Franciscan Order. He died while he was assisting at the Second Council of Lyons, on July 15, 1274, and was canonized in 1482 by Pope Sixtus IV.

PRAYER: *Almighty God, today we celebrate the heavenly birthday of St. Bonaventure, Your Bishop. Let us benefit by his wonderful teaching and always be inspired by his burning charity.*

SAINT BONIFACE

Bishop and Martyr

June 5

ST. BONIFACE, whose baptismal name was Winfrid, was born about the year 680 in Devonshire, England. From the age of thirteen he was educated in the Benedictine monastery of Exeter, where he later became a monk. He then moved on to the abbey of Nursling in the diocese of Winchester, which enjoyed a great reputation for learning. After some time the Abbot appointed Boniface to teach. At the age of thirty he was ordained to the priesthood.

With the permission of his Abbot, Boniface went to Friesland in Holland in 716, in order to preach to the idolaters. His first attempt was unfortunately unsuccessful, and he was obliged to return to England, where he was chosen Abbot of his monastery, a dignity that he soon decided to resign.

In 719, he went to Rome and presented himself to Pope Gregory II, begging authority to preach to the idolaters. The Pope, having seen the letters of his Bishop, gave to Boniface ample power to preach the Faith to the heathens in Germany.

While in Germany, he destroyed the temples of idols and built churches. A story is told that once Boniface cut down a huge oak that was dedicated to the god Jupiter and then used the tree in building a church dedicated to St. Peter.

In 745, more than twenty years after Pope Gregory II ordained him Bishop and after he had established a number of dioceses in Germany, the Saint chose Mainz as his Episcopal See. He ended his fruitful career by a glorious martyrdom in Friesland, where he had returned to preach the Faith. He and fifty-two Christians who were with him died at the hands of a troop of pagans. Their deaths occurred on June 5, 754.

PRAYER: *Lord, let St. Boniface intercede for us, that we may firmly adhere to the Faith he taught, and for which he shed his blood, and fearlessly profess it in our works.*

~ Apostle of Germany ~

~ Patroness of Sweden ~

SAINT BRIDGET
Religious
July 23

S T. BRIDGET was the daughter of a royal Prince of Sweden, named Birger, and of Inge-burdis, a descendant of the Gothic Kings. From these pious parents she inherited a great love for the Passion of our Lord. Her father consecrated all Fridays to special acts of penance, and from her childhood St. Bridget loved to meditate upon the Passion of Christ. In obedience to her father, at the age of sixteen she married Ulfo, Prince of Nericia in Sweden, by whom she had eight children, the last of whom, Catherine, is now honored among the Saints.

Later the holy couple bound themselves by a vow of chastity and made a pilgrimage to Compostela in Galicia. On their return to Sweden, Ulfo, with his wife's consent, entered a Cistercian monastery, where he died soon after, wearing a mantle of sanctity. After his death St. Bridget re-nounced her rank of princess and changed her habit.

In 1344, she built the great monastery of Wastein, which became the motherhouse of a new Order that she founded, the Order of Saint Savior, or the Brigittines. She next undertook a pilgrimage to Rome and to Palestine. Having satisfied her devotion at the holy places sanctified by the life and Passion of our Redeemer, she returned to Rome, where she lived a year longer.

During this time she was sorely afflicted by sickness, but endured it with heroic patience and resignation for the love of Jesus on the Cross. Her son, Birger, and her daughter, Catherine, were with her in her last moments. Having given them her final instructions, she received the Last Sacraments and died in 1373. Canonized in 1391, she is remembered for her visions, composed in Swedish and translated into Latin.

PRAYER: *Lord God, You revealed heavenly secrets to St. Bridget as she meditated on the Passion of Your Son. Grant that we Your servants may attain the joyful contemplation of Your glory.*

SAINT CATHERINE OF SIENA

Virgin and Doctor of the Church

April 29

ST. CATHERINE, the most remarkable woman of her age, was born in 1347. In her childhood she consecrated her virginity to God. However her parents, wishing to see her married, began to thwart her pious inclinations. She finally became an object of persecution in her own house. She bore her trials with fortitude and joy, persevering in her resolution of giving herself entirely to the Divine service. Eventually her parents relented, and she was left free to follow her pious inclinations.

In 1365, at eighteen, she received the habit of the Third Order of St. Dominic. In 1374, during the great pestilence, she devoted herself heroically to the care of the infected. Meanwhile, she was considered to be a power for good, since thousands were converted by her exhortations.

Two years later she went to Avignon to intercede with the Pope for the Florentines, who had been interdicted for joining in a conspiracy against the temporal possessions of the Holy See in Italy. She aided Gregory XI's return to Rome, and she exhorted him to contribute, by all possible means, toward the peace of Italy.

Having lived to see the beginning of the great schism, she wrote to the cardinals who were the cause of it and to several princes, seeking to avert the terrible evil. The life of the Saint who had been glorified by God with wondrous gifts and miracles was brought to a close on April 29, 1380, at the age of thirty-three. She was canonized in 1461 by Pope Pius II.

St. Catherine has long been regarded as one of the finest theological minds in the Church—as is shown by her outstanding work, *Dialogue*—and in 1970 Pope Paul VI declared her a Doctor of the Church.

PRAYER: *God, You caused St. Catherine to shine with Divine love in the contemplation of the Lord's Passion and in the service of Your Church. By her help, grant that Your people, associated in the mystery of Christ, may ever exult in the revelation of His glory.*

~ Patroness of Fire Prevention ~

~ Patroness of Musicians ~

SAINT CECILIA
Virgin and Martyr

November 22

ACCORDING to her legendary Acts, Cecilia was a native of Rome, born of patrician parents who raised her as a Christian. At an early age she made a vow of virginity, but her parents forced her to marry a Roman nobleman named Valerian. By the Providence of God, although married, she preserved her virginity. Furthermore, through her example, she converted her husband to the Faith of Christ, and he was baptized by Pope Urban.

She also converted Tiburtius, the brother of Valerian. During the persecution of Christians, the two brothers secretly buried martyrs. Both of these men suffered martyrdom themselves for the Faith, and St. Cecilia died in the same manner a few days after them. Their deaths occurred probably in the reign of either Marcus Aurelius or Commodus, sometime between the years 161 and 192.

The circumstances surrounding the death of St. Cecilia have been drawn from legend. Ever dedicated to the Faith, she refused to sacrifice to the gods when challenged to do so by local authorities. She was to be put to death either by smothering or by being placed in a caldron of boiling water, but the hand of God protected His servant. When this means did not work, a soldier was told to behead her. Although he struck her three times, she was badly wounded but remained alive for another three days. Only after receiving Holy Communion one last time did she succumb to death.

The name of St. Cecilia has always been most illustrious in the Church because she is held as one of the most famous and most loved of the Roman martyrs. Since primitive ages, her name has been mentioned in the Canon of the Mass (the First Eucharistic Prayer). She is honored as the patroness of ecclesiastical music and is often depicted with some type of musical instrument in various art forms.

PRAYER: *Lord, hear our requests. Through the intercession of St. Cecilia, please grant what we ask.*

SAINT CHARLES BORROMEO

Bishop

ST. CHARLES, of the noble family of Borromeo, was born in 1538 on the banks of Lake Maggiore, Italy. He studied at Milan and afterward at the University of Pavia, where he received his doctorate in civil and canon law in 1559. His uncle, the Cardinal de Medici, having in the same year been elected Pope under the title of Pius IV, sent for him and created him Cardinal, and a short time afterward nominated him Archbishop of Milan, though he was only twenty-two years of age.

At that time he was detained at Rome by the Pope and he began to labor diligently in Church interests. There he founded the Vatican Academy for literary work. As Papal Secretary of State he was instrumental in reassembling the Council of Trent in 1562. He was active in enforcing its reforms and in composing the Roman Catechism, containing the teachings of the Council.

After receiving priestly ordination, he also accepted the office of grand penitentiary. For merely honorary or lucrative positions he had no ambition. He assisted at the deathbed of the Pope in 1564, and on the election of Pius V he went to reside at Milan.

Although he was deeply involved in the high-level inner workings of the Church, he worked tirelessly to reach out to people who needed his help in their everyday lives. He founded schools for the poor, seminaries for clerics, and through his community of Oblates trained priests in living lives of holiness. This Saint also built hospitals where he personally served the sick.

In 1572, he concurred in the election of Gregory XIII. In the great plague at Milan, in 1575, he showed himself the true shepherd by his self-sacrificing charity and heroism. This great light in the firmament of the Church was extinguished in 1584, at the age of forty-six. He was canonized in 1610 by Pope Paul V.

PRAYER: *God, maintain in Your people that spirit with which You inspired Your Bishop, St. Charles, so that Your Church may be constantly renewed, conforming itself to Christ and manifesting Christ to the world.*

~ Patron of Seminarians ~

~ Patron of Motorists ~

SAINT CHRISTOPHER

Martyr

ST. CHRISTOPHER is one of the most popular Saints of the East and West. There are many legends concerning this Saint that are often confused and contradictory.

A composite story of the legends surrounding him tells of a very strong man (some say he might even have been a giant) named Offero who lived in the land of Canaan in Palestine. Apparently, he felt compelled to leave his home and search out adventure throughout the world.

It was his goal to serve the mightiest of kings. Initially, he believed the devil to be the mightiest, but he then discovered that the devil feared Christ. He then decided that it was Christ Whom he must serve.

While on his journeys, he came upon a hermit who guarded a dangerous passage across a stream. This hermit guided travelers to a place where they could safely cross the stream. Even more importantly, the hermit taught Offero about Christ, the greatest King. Finding this spot an appealing one, Offero settled there and carried travelers across the stream on his shoulders in order to well serve the great King.

As legends have it, one day he carried a small boy upon his shoulders. He was amazed at the weight of the little child and told the young boy that he felt as if it were the entire world he bore. In response, the small child told him that, rather than carrying the whole world, Offero was carrying Him Who created both heaven and earth. Legends go on to say that the boy Jesus baptized Offero, and, from then on, he was to be called Christopher, that is, Christ-bearer.

He is the patron of travelers, particularly motorists, and is invoked against storms, plagues, and other dangers. It is said that he died a martyr during the reign of Decius in the third century.

PRAYER: *Almighty and ever-living God, graciously pour out Your Spirit upon us. Let our hearts be filled with that true love that enabled Your holy Martyr Christopher to overcome all bodily torments.*

SAINT CLARE

Virgin

August 11

ASSISI, the birthplace of St. Francis, had also the honor of being the place where St. Clare, his spiritual daughter, was born in 1193. From her childhood she desired to consecrate herself to Jesus Christ. Having heard of St. Francis and his sanctity, she contrived to be taken to him by a pious matron. The conversation of St. Francis made her resolve to abandon the world. On March 18, 1212, she and another young woman went to the Portiuncula, where St. Francis prayed, and received the penitential habit.

At first St. Francis placed her in a Benedictine convent of nuns. She persevered in her resolution, in spite of the opposition of her friends and relatives. Later her sister Agnes joined her. St. Francis then placed them in a separate house. Soon after, her mother and several other ladies, some of high nobility, united themselves to her. The foundation of Poor Clares, or the Second Order of St. Francis, was thus laid. Within a few years St. Clare founded a number of other monasteries and her Order spread to Germany and Bohemia.

The austerities these religious women practiced had scarcely ever been known among their gender. Together with other mortifications, their fast was perpetual. Such was the spirit of poverty of St. Clare that when, after her profession, she fell heiress to the large fortune of her father, she gave all of it to the poor. She would accept no revenues for her monastery.

When the army of Frederick II was devastating the valley of Spoleto some of the soldiers placed a ladder against the convent wall. St. Clare caused herself to be carried to a window, and, holding the monstrance with the Blessed Sacrament in sight of the enemies, she prostrated herself before the Eucharistic God. Her prayer was heard, and the enemies, struck with a sudden panic, fled in terror. St. Clare died on August 11, 1253. She was canonized in 1255 by Pope Alexander IV.

PRAYER: *God, in Your mercy You led St. Clare to embrace poverty. Through her intercession help us to follow Christ in the spirit of poverty and to contemplate You in the heavenly Kingdom.*

~ *Patroness of Television* ~

~ *Patron of Astronomers* ~

SAINT DOMINIC

Priest

ST. DOMINIC, a native of Calaroga in Old Castile, Spain, was of the illustrious house of the Guzmans. At the age of fourteen he was sent to the schools of Valencia, which were soon after transferred to Salamanca. Having finished his education, he received the habit of the Regular Canons of St. Augustine in the diocese of Osma. Devoting himself with ardor to the work of his own sanctification, he also labored for the salvation of others by preaching the Word of God.

He accompanied his Bishop on a mission imposed by Alphonsus IX, King of Castile. In France they became acquainted with the ravages of the Albigensian heresy. Both the Bishop and his companion proceeded to Rome, where they obtained permission from Innocent III to preach the Gospel among the heretics. They now began to labor with great zeal. To provide for the education of children, St. Dominic established a convent of nuns at Prouille, which became the nucleus of the Order of Dominican nuns. St. Dominic succeeded the Bishop of Osma as superior of the missions in Languedoc. Together with several companions of his labors, he laid the foundations of his Order, the Rules of which were approved by Pope Honorius III in 1216.

Sometime later, the Pope created the office of Master of the Sacred Palace (the Pope's domestic theologian), and St. Dominic was the first to fill it. The Saint spent time traveling for the interests of God and His Church: preaching the Gospel, lecturing on theology, and establishing houses of his Order. These houses, of which Honorius III made him General in 1220, made great progress during Dominic's lifetime. His saintly life was happily terminated at Bologna, Italy, August 6, 1221, and he was canonized in 1234 by Pope Gregory IX. The Saint is frequently pictured with a dog holding a torch in its mouth, symbolizing the fire of his zeal for souls.

PRAYER: *God, let St. Dominic help Your Church by his merits and teaching. May he who was an outstanding preacher of truth become a most generous intercessor for us.*

SAINT ELIZABETH ANN SETON

Religious

ELIZABETH SETON was born on August 28, 1774, to a wealthy and distinguished Episcopalian family, probably at Trinity Church in New York City. She lost her mother at an early age, leaving her upbringing and education to the discretion of her father. She was a voracious reader and truly enjoyed the Bible. In her youth and young adulthood, Elizabeth was a faithful, fervent adherent of the Episcopal Church until her conversion to Catholicism.

In 1794, at nineteen, Elizabeth married William Magee Seton, also of New York. Although this union was a happy one that produced five children, their life together was plagued by suffering and illness. Elizabeth and her sick husband traveled to Leghorn, Italy, in the hope that the location would help his condition improve. Unfortunately, it was there that William died.

While in Italy, trying to recover from the loss of her husband, Elizabeth was comforted by life-long friends, the Filicchis, who helped acquaint her with Catholicism. It was in 1805 that she joined the Catholic Church.

Elizabeth was invited to establish her first Catholic school in Baltimore in 1808; this was the beginning of the parochial school system in America. Then in 1809 she established a religious community in Emmitsburg, Maryland, soon becoming known as Mother Seton. Her small community of teaching sisters grew and expanded throughout the country, eventually becoming the Sisters of Charity.

Tuberculosis took her life on January 4, 1821. She was beatified in 1963 and then was canonized on September 14, 1975, by Pope Paul VI, making her the first American-born Saint.

PRAYER: *God, You raised up St. Elizabeth in Your Church so that she might instruct others in the way of salvation. Grant that we may follow Christ after her example and may reach You in the company of our brothers and sisters.*

~ *First American-born Saint* ~

~ Patroness of Immigrants ~

SAINT FRANCES XAVIER CABRINI

Virgin

November 13

FRANCES XAVIER CABRINI was born in Lombardy, Italy, in 1850, the youngest of thirteen children. At eighteen, she desired to become a Sister, but poor health stood in her way. She helped her parents until their deaths in 1870, and then worked on a farm with her brothers and sisters.

One day a priest asked her to teach in a girls' school, and she stayed for six years. At the request of her Bishop, she founded the Missionary Sisters of the Sacred Heart to care for poor children in schools and hospitals. Then, at the urging of Pope Leo XIII, she went to the United States with six Sisters in 1889 to work among the numerous Italian immigrants who had gone to America's shores.

Filled with a deep trust in God and endowed with a wonderful administrative ability, this remarkable woman soon founded schools, hospitals, and orphanages in a foreign land and saw them flourish, providing much-needed aid to great numbers of Italian immigrants and children. All totaled, Frances Xavier Cabrini founded sixty-seven institutions dedicated to caring for the poor, the abandoned, the uneducated, and the sick. She was called "Mother" because of her selfless care of so many. In order to accomplish her far-reaching work, she overcame a childhood fear of water and traveled across the seas more than thirty times.

At the time of her death from malaria on December 22, 1917, in Chicago, her institute numbered houses in England, France, Spain, the United States, and South America. On July 7, 1946, she became the first American citizen (having become a United States citizen in 1909) to be canonized, when she was elevated to Sainthood by Pope Pius XII.

PRAYER: *God, through the work of St. Frances Cabrini you brought comfort and love to the immigrants and those in need. May her example and work be continued in the lives of those dedicated to You.*

SAINT FRANCIS OF ASSISI

October 4

FRANCIS BERNARDONE, the founder of the three Franciscan Orders, was born at Assisi, Italy, in 1181. His father was a wealthy merchant of the town. During a year's imprisonment at Perugia due to his participation as a knight in an unsuccessful campaign against that town, and again during a prolonged severe illness, Francis became aware of a vocation to a life of extraordinary service to the Church of Christ.

Inspired at the age of twenty-five by the Scripture passage of Matthew commanding the disciples to evangelize the world without possessions, Francis abandoned his affluent way of life and began to live a life of radical poverty. Disinherited by his father, Francis went away penniless "to wed Lady Poverty" and to live a life that was poorer than the poor whom he served. His example soon drew followers to his way of life.

Three years later, in 1210, with twelve companions, he sought and received the approval of Pope Innocent III to lead a life according to the Rule of the Holy Gospel, and they became a band of roving preachers of Christ in simplicity and lowliness. Thus began the "Friars Minor," or "Lesser Brothers." Up and down the extent of Italy the brothers summoned the people to faith and penitence; they refused even corporate ownership of property, human learning, and ecclesiastical preferment. St. Francis himself never became a priest out of humility, and at first only some of his band were in Holy Orders.

Francis's practice of evangelical poverty and devotion to the humanity of Christ warmed the hearts of a "world growing cold" and soon a vast Franciscan movement was sweeping through Europe. By 1219, over five thousand Franciscans gathered at Assisi for the famed Chapter of Mats. To accommodate this religious revival, Francis founded a Second Order through St. Clare of Assisi for cloistered nuns and a Third Order for religious and laity of both sexes.

Francis died at sunset on October 3, 1226, and was canonized two years later.

PRAYER: *God, You enabled St. Francis to imitate Christ by his poverty and humility. Walking in St. Francis's footsteps, may we follow Your Son and be bound to You by a joyful love.*

~ *Patron of Catholic Action* ~

~ Patron of Writers ~

SAINT FRANCIS DE SALES

Bishop and Doctor of the Church

ST. FRANCIS, son of the Count de Sales, was born near Annecy in Savoy, in 1567. Showing an early inclination for the ecclesiastical state he received tonsure at eleven years of age. Soon afterward, he was sent to Paris to study philosophy and theology. He went on to the University of Padua where he was honored with a doctorate in both canon and civil law.

On his return home, with the reluctant consent of his parents, Francis entered the priesthood. A little later, he took upon himself the arduous mission of Chablais, where Calvinism had obtained a stronghold. In the midst of the most enormous difficulties, he pursued his labors with apostolic heroism, and was rewarded with the most wonderful fruits of conversion. While engaged in this work he received his appointment as coadjutor to the Bishop of Geneva, whom he succeeded as Bishop in 1602.

He labored zealously in his diocese for the clergy and people, and extended his labors elsewhere, preaching the Lenten sermons at various places outside of the diocese. He also composed several instructive works for the edification of the faithful. In 1610 he founded the Order of the Visitation, with the help of the Baroness de Chantal, now St. Jane Frances.

Amid his constant pastoral work Francis found time to write the book that has made him known to succeeding ages: *Introduction to a Devout Life* (1609). It shows how ordinary life can be sanctified; no problem is too small for its author: dress, entertainments, flirtations, etc. His one concern is how to lead the reader to the love of God and the imitation of Christ.

In an age when fanaticism was the rule in controversies, Francis manifested an exceptional restraint and meekness. His pastoral zeal, which was anxious for the sanctification of the laity and the adaptation of the religious life to the new needs, marks a turning point in the history of spirituality. He died in 1622 with the word "Jesus" on his lips, and was canonized in 1665 by Pope Alexander VII.

PRAYER: *Father in heaven, You prompted St. Francis de Sales to become all things to all for the salvation of all. May his example inspire us to dedicated love in the service of our brothers and sisters.*

SAINT FRANCIS XAVIER

Priest

December 3

THE Apostle of the Indies was born at the castle of Xavier in Navarre, Spain, in 1506. He was of noble descent. At the age of eighteen he went to Paris to study philosophy. About four years later, St. Ignatius Loyola came to the same city and took up his abode in the College of St. Barbara, to which St. Francis belonged. At that time St. Francis was full of the world and ambition, but the company of St. Ignatius exercised such a beneficent influence upon him that he became a changed man and one of the Saint's first disciples.

In 1536, he went to Venice with the first companions of St. Ignatius. After visiting Rome he was ordained a priest at Venice in 1537, and the first Jesuits made their vows before the Pope's nuncio. Shortly after the Society had been established, St. Francis was sent to Portugal. In 1541, he set sail for India, which was to be the field of his labors for the rest of his life, and landed at Goa the following year. From that city, which he completely reformed, his apostolic labors extended to the coast of Malabar, to Travancor, Malacca, the Moluccas, and Ceylon, and in all these places he converted large numbers to Christianity.

In 1549, he carried the light of Faith to Japan, of which he became the first missionary, and where a flourishing Christian community soon arose. He remained in Japan two years and four months, and returned to India in 1551.

He then turned his eyes to China. After visiting Goa, he set sail, in 1552, to carry out his resolve, but God was satisfied with his will. On the twenty-third day after his departure from Malacca he arrived at Sancian. On November 20 a fever seized him, and, alone upon a foreign shore, he died on Friday, December 2, 1552, at the age of forty-six. He was canonized in 1602 by Pope Clement VIII.

PRAYER: *Lord, You won many peoples for Your Church through the preaching of St. Francis. Inspire the faithful today with the same zeal for spreading the Faith, so that everywhere the Church might rejoice in her many children.*

~ Patron of Foreign Missions ~

~ *Patron of Communications Workers* ~

SAINT GABRIEL

Archangel

September 29

ANGELS are spirits without bodies, who possess superior intelligence, gigantic strength, and surpassing holiness. They enjoy an intimate relationship to God as His special adopted children, contemplating, loving, and praising Him in heaven. Some of them are often sent to earth as messengers to people from on high.

The name Gabriel means "man of God," or "God has shown Himself mighty." His name is first mentioned in the Bible in the Book of Daniel. In chapter 8 (verses 17–26), he explains a vision Daniel had, a vision that referred to the time when God would pass judgment on His enemies. In the next chapter (9:21–27), Gabriel explains the prophecy of the seventy weeks, which referred to Christ being the ultimate realization and definitive establishment of God's kingdom.

Besides these Old Testament appearances, Gabriel played an important role in announcing the births of two children in the Gospel of Luke in the New Testament. It was Gabriel who appeared to Zechariah in the sanctuary during the course of Zechariah's priestly service to tell him of the birth of John the Baptist, a son who would be set aside for the Lord's service (Luke 1:11–20). When Zechariah did not believe the Angel's message, Gabriel told him that he would not be able to speak until his son was born.

Gabriel's greatest message was delivered to Mary in Nazareth (Luke 1:26–38), when he announced to her that she would bear a Son Who would be conceived of the Holy Spirit, Son of the Most High, and the Savior of the world.

It is Gabriel's words of greeting to Mary that we still say today in the opening words of the Hail Mary. He heralded her as being full of grace and declared her and the Fruit of her womb as blessed.

This accounts for the fact that Gabriel's feast was formerly kept on March 24, the day before the feast of the Annunciation. In the post-Vatican II Roman Missal, his feast has been transferred and is now celebrated on September 29 together with the feasts of Sts. Michael and Raphael, the other two Angels mentioned in the Bible.

PRAYER: *God, with great wisdom You direct the ministry of Angels and people. Grant that those who always minister to You in heaven may defend us during our life on earth.*

SAINT GREGORY THE GREAT

Pope and Doctor of the Church

September 3

ST. GREGORY, born at Rome about the year 540, was the son of St. Silvia and Gordianus, a wealthy senator, who later renounced the world and became one of the seven deacons of Rome. After Gregory had acquired the usual thorough education, Emperor Justin the Younger appointed him, in 574, Chief Magistrate of Rome, though he was only thirty-four years of age.

After the death of his father he built six monasteries in Sicily on estates he owned and founded a seventh in his own house in Rome, which became the Benedictine Monastery of St. Andrew. Here he himself assumed the monastic habit in 575, at the age of thirty-five. For a certain period of time, he served as abbot of St. Andrew's.

After the death of Pope Pelagius from the plague, St. Gregory was elected Pope and elevated to the papacy in September of 590. It is the way he conducted himself and the duties of his position that merited for him the title of "the Great." He brought reform to questionable practices in the Church, extended much-needed support to charities, sought justice for the imprisoned and abused, and initiated the practice of temporal power by the papacy. He played a significant part in converting England to Christianity, with the assistance of St. Augustine and a company of monks from St. Andrew's, whom he sent there. In addition, he was an ardent and active proponent of the papacy as the Church's supreme authority.

Gregory is widely known for his numerous writings, and, most especially, for his contributions to the Roman liturgy. Gregorian Chant bears his name. He is honored as one of the four great Doctors of the Latin Church. Gregory, the Apostle of the English, died on March 12, 604, in Rome.

PRAYER: *God, You look upon Your people with compassion and rule them with love. Through the intercession of Pope St. Gregory, give wisdom to the leaders of Your Church.*

~ *Patron of Teachers* ~

perinde ac ■■■adaver

~ *Patron of Retreats* ~

SAINT IGNATIUS LOYOLA

Priest

July 31

ST. IGNATIUS was born of a noble family in 1491, in the Castle of Loyola in Guipuscoa, Spain. Reared in the Court of Ferdinand V of Aragon, the husband of Isabella of Castile, he entered the army and distinguished himself by his valor. He was wounded at the siege of Pamplona, in a war between Charles V and Francis I, King of France. During his convalescence he read the "Lives of the Saints" which effected his conversion from worldliness to piety. Henceforth, his life belonged entirely to God.

After a general confession in the monastery of Montserrat, he spent ten months in the solitude of Manresa, where he composed his *Spiritual Exercises*, which draw from the traditional teaching of the abbey of Montserrat, and then made a pilgrimage to Rome and the Holy Land. On his return to Spain he began his studies, and in 1528 he went to Paris to continue them. Here his virtue and wisdom gained him a few companions, and these became the nucleus of the Society of Jesus. At Montmartre they vowed to go to Palestine, or to offer themselves to the Pope to be employed in the service of God in some other manner. Receiving ordination at Venice together with his companions, St. Ignatius went to Rome where he was graciously received by Pope Paul III.

In 1540, Pope Paul III approved the Society and it soon made rapid progress, spreading to India in the East and to Brazil in the West. St. Ignatius continued to reside in Rome, employed in consolidating and governing his Society. There he became the friend of St. Philip Neri. He was General of the Society more than fifteen years. He died peacefully on July 31, 1556, and was canonized in 1622 by Pope Gregory XV.

St. Ignatius's legacy lies both in his famous *Exercises* and in the education provided by Jesuit schools.

PRAYER: *God, You raised up St. Ignatius in Your Church to inspire people to work for Your greater glory. Grant that we may labor on earth with his help and after his example and merit be crowned with him in heaven.*

SAINT ISAAC JOGUES

Priest and Martyr

October 19

STS. ISAAC JOGUES, John de Brebeuf, Charles Garmier, Anthony Daniel, Gabriel Lallemant, Noel Chabanel, John de Lalande and René Goupil, French Jesuits, were among the missionaries who preached the Gospel to Huron and Iroquois Indians in the United States and Canada. They were martyred by the Iroquois Indians in the years 1642, 1646, 1648, and 1649. Pope Pius XI beatified them on June 21, 1925, and in 1930 they were canonized by the same Pope.

St. Isaac Jogues, in particular, is outstanding. He was born at Orleans, France, in 1607, and left fatherless while still an infant. Little else is known of his early life until he was ordained in Rouen in 1624. In the course of his labors preaching the Gospel to the Mohawks in Canada, an endeavor he began in 1636, he penetrated to the eastern entrance of Lake Superior, one thousand miles inland and became the first European to do so. In 1642, he was taken captive by the Iroquois and imprisoned for thirteen months. During this time, he underwent cruel tortures and ultimately lost the use of his hands. After being rescued by the Dutch, he returned to Canada two years later, and in 1646 he visited Auriesville, New York, to negotiate peace with the Iroquois. He is said to be the first Catholic priest to have set foot on Manhattan Island.

On Isaac's third visit to the Iroquois, the Bear clan, which believed that he was a sorcerer because of a box of religious objects he had left behind, blamed him for an outbreak of sickness and the failure of their crops. Accordingly, this "Apostle of the Mohawks" was seized, tortured, and beheaded.

PRAYER: *God, You consecrated the spread of the Faith in North America by the blood of St. Isaac Jogues and his companions. Through their intercession let more people everywhere respond to the Good News of salvation.*

~ North American Martyr ~

~ *National Saint of Spain* ~

SAINT ISIDORE OF SEVILLE

Bishop and Doctor of the Church

April 4

ST. ISIDORE was born at Cartagena in Spain, the son of Severinus and Theodora, illustrious for their virtue. St. Leander and St. Fulgentius, both Bishops, were his brothers, and his sister, Florentina, is also numbered among the Saints.

From his youth Isidore consecrated himself to the service of the Church and prepared himself for his sacred ministry by virtue and learning. He assisted his brother St. Leander, Archbishop of Seville, in the conversion of the Visigoths from the Arian heresy. On his brother's death, about the year 600, he succeeded him in the See of Seville.

Several Councils at which he assisted settled the discipline of the Spanish Church, and in that of Seville, in 619, he converted Gregory, a Eutychian Bishop from Syria. A few years before, in 610, the Archbishop of Toledo, in a Council held at Toledo, had been declared Primate of all Spain. Notwithstanding this, the personal merit of St. Isidore was so highly esteemed that he presided at the Fourth Council of Toledo, held in 633, although the Primate was present. This Council was the most famous of all the Spanish synods. At that time Toledo was the capital of Spain and the residence of the Visigothic kings.

St. Isidore was also a voluminous writer. He composed a work containing the whole circle of science, which shows his vast erudition. This is one of the earliest encyclopedias on record. The Saint was versed in the Latin, Greek, and Hebrew languages.

Isidore governed his church about thirty-seven years, continuing his assiduous labors up to a most advanced age. During the last six months of his life his charities became more profuse than ever. Perceiving his end approaching he went to church, received Holy Communion, remitted all the debts that were due to him, and caused his money to be distributed to the poor. He then returned home and calmly expired four days later, in 636.

> PRAYER: *Lord, hear our prayers, which we offer on the commemoration of St. Isidore. May Your Church be instructed by his teaching.*

SAINT JAMES THE GREATER

Apostle

July 25

THIS Saint is usually called "the Greater" in order to distinguish him from the other Apostle James, the "brother" of the Lord, who is called "the Less." He was the brother of St. John the Evangelist (sons of Zebedee and Salome) and came from Bethsaida in Galilee, where his father owned a fishing boat.

The two youths were fishing with their father when Jesus came by and invited them to follow Him. They became such dedicated and zealous followers that our Lord styled them *Boanerges*, or sons of thunder. They were present at the cure of St. Peter's mother-in-law, the raising of Jairus's daughter, and the Transfiguration, and were near Christ in His Agony in the Garden.

One day their mother asked Jesus to assure a place of honor for her sons in His future Kingdom. When He asked if they were able to bear the cup of His sufferings, their answer was typical of them: indeed they could! Jesus told them that they would drink of the cup that He was to drink. But it was for the Father to say who would sit on His left and right in His Kingdom.

James was also one of the four Apostles who put questions to Jesus concerning the last things during the Lord's address on the Mount of Olives as they stood overlooking the Temple. Finally, he was present when the Risen Jesus appeared to the disciples and the miraculous catch of fish occurred at the Sea of Tiberias.

After the dispersion of the Apostles, St. James preached the Gospel in Spain and then returned to Jerusalem, where he was the first of the Apostles to drink the cup of Christ's sufferings. By order of Herod Agrippa he was beheaded at Jerusalem around the feast of Easter, in the year 44.

PRAYER: *Almighty, ever-living God, through the blood of St. James You consecrated the first fruits of the ministry of Your Apostles. Grant that Your Church may be strengthened by his confession and always enjoy his patronage.*

~ Patron of Laborers ~

~ Patroness of Educators ~

SAINT JANE FRANCES DE CHANTAL

Religious

August 12

BORN at Dijon in 1572, into a prominent family, St. Jane Frances received an excellent education. In 1592, she married the Baron de Chantal, an officer in the army of Henry IV. After eight happy years, she was left a widow with four little children when the Baron was killed in a hunting accident. He died in the arms of his disconsolate wife, whom he left a widow at the age of twenty-eight with one little son and three daughters.

The young widow now gave herself entirely to God and to the exercises of religion. In 1604, she heard St. Francis de Sales preach and placed herself under his spiritual direction. Realizing that she felt called to the religious life, St. Francis told her of a new congregation that he intended to form.

St. Jane Frances put her affairs in order and made provision for her children. Then in 1610 she along with three other women began the Congregation of the Visitation under the direction of St. Francis.

This congregation was especially for those women called to the religious life who wanted to follow a different type of vocation from the older forms available at the time. It was for the members of this new congregation that St. Francis wrote his spiritual classic *On the Love of God*.

St. Francis died in 1622, but St. Jane Frances survived him by nearly twenty years. During the remainder of her life, she continued to direct her religious in the spirit with which St. Francis had imbued her.

For many years she suffered great interior trials with the utmost resignation, while she labored to extend her Congregation and promote God's glory. Eighty-six houses were established before her death in 1641. She was canonized in 1767 by Pope Clement XIII.

PRAYER: *God, You endowed St. Jane Frances with admirable qualities in various walks of life. Through her intercession help us to be true to our vocation and never fail to bear witness to the light You give us.*

SAINT JEROME

Priest and Doctor of the Church

September 30

STRIDONIUM, a small town on the border of Dalmatia, was the place where St. Jerome was born about 347. In Rome he studied Latin and Greek, devoted himself to oratory, and pleaded at the bar. For a time he gave himself up to the world, but his piety returned to him after he began to travel.

Having made a tour of Gaul, he went again to Rome, there receiving Baptism, which at that time was frequently deferred until a mature age. From Rome, he journeyed to the East, and visited the Anchorites and other persons of sanctity.

After sojourning a while at Antioch, he took up his abode in the desert of Chalcis in Syria, with the holy Abbot Theodosius. Here he spent four years of prayer and study, including the study of Hebrew.

At Antioch he received Holy Orders about the year 377, under the stipulation that he should not be obliged to serve in the ministry. After traveling in Palestine, he visited Constantinople, where St. Gregory Nazianzen was then Bishop. Again returning to Palestine, he departed for Rome, where he filled for some time the office of secretary to Pope St. Damasus, who asked him to revise the Latin versions of the Bible that were current at the time. This project took St. Jerome from 385 to 405 and resulted in the *Vulgate* (i.e., the text in general use), which became the official Latin version of the Bible for the Catholic Church.

After the death of St. Damasus, he returned to the East, in 385. On his way he visited St. Epiphanius at Cyprus, and arrived at Jerusalem in the winter, leaving soon after for Alexandria to improve himself in sacred learning. Returning to Palestine, he retired to Bethlehem, where his solitary life began the career of study that has immortalized him.

Jerome's scriptural works, above all, have been unparalleled. He also attacked the various errors of his day. His fame spread far and wide, and people came to consult him from all sides. He also governed and directed the monastery of nuns founded by St. Paula. After a long life of prayer, penance, and labor, he died at Bethlehem in 420.

PRAYER: *God, You gave St. Jerome a great love for Holy Scripture. Let Your people feed more abundantly on Your Word and find in it the source of life.*

~ Patron of Librarians ~

~ *Husband of Saint Anne* ~

SAINT JOACHIM

Father of Mary

July 26

ST. JOACHIM has been honored from time immemorial in the Churches of the East, and since the 6th century public devotion to him has been observed in all countries. From 1622 on, he has shared a joint feast on July 26 with his wife Anne. Their feast is considered as primarily not in honor of Saints but in honor of Jesus, the Redeemer, of Whom they are the grandparents.

As is true of St. Anne, the New Testament tells us nothing about Joachim. Tradition, grounded on very old testimonies, informs us that Sts. Joachim and Anne in their old age came to settle in Jerusalem. They were childless and suffered the scorn that was associated with this situation in their day.

A fervent couple, known for their charity, they gave alms for the poor and for the upkeep of the Temple, and only then did they take care of their own needs. Scriptural parallels have been applied to both. Joachim is likened to the just man of Psalm 111 and the charitable Tobit (in chapters 4 and 12). Anne is represented as the model wife and valiant woman of Proverbs chapter 31.

The story goes that because of their childlessness Joachim is turned away by a priest in the Temple when he comes to offer sacrifice. In desperation Joachim leaves his wife so that he may make amends for any sin he may have committed that brought on his disgrace. He lives in solitude with the shepherds and their flocks.

At the same time, Anne is praying that God may lift her burden and grant her a child.

An Angel tells Joachim that Anne is going to bear a daughter for him and orders him to go to the Golden Gate at Jerusalem. The same Angel tells Anne to go to the Golden Gate to be united with her husband. The two holy people promise to give their child, Mary, to the Lord. At the age of three, Mary is brought to the Temple to remain there as a temple virgin.

Sts. Joachim and Anne died in Jerusalem, and a church was built during the fourth century—possibly by St. Helena—on the site of their home in Jerusalem.

> PRAYER: *Lord, God of our fathers, through St. Joachim You gave us the Mother of Your Incarnate Son. May his prayers help us to attain the salvation You promised to Your people.*

SAINT JOAN OF ARC

Virgin

May 30

ON January 6, 1412, Joan of Arc was born to pious parents of the French peasant class, at the obscure village of Domremy, near the province of Lorraine. At a very early age she heard voices: those of St. Michael, St. Catherine, and St. Margaret.

At first the messages were personal and general. Then at last came the crowning order. In May 1428, her voices told Joan to go to the King of France and help him reconquer his kingdom. For at that time the English King was after the throne of France, and the Duke of Burgundy (the chief rival of the French King) was siding with him and gobbling up ever more French territory.

After overcoming opposition from churchmen and courtiers, the seventeen-year-old girl was given a small army with which she raised the siege of Orleans on May 8, 1429. She then enjoyed a series of spectacular military successes, during which the King was able to enter Rheims and be crowned with her at his side.

In May 1430, as Joan was attempting to relieve Compiégne, she was captured by the Burgundians and sold to the English when Charles and the French did nothing to save her. After months of imprisonment, she was tried at Rouen by a tribunal presided over by the infamous Peter Cauchon, Bishop of Beauvais, who hoped that the English would help him to become Archbishop.

Through her unfamiliarity with the technicalities of theology, Joan was trapped into making a few damaging statements. When she refused to retract the assertion that it was the Saints of God who had commanded her to do what she had done, she was condemned to death as a heretic, sorceress, and adulteress, and burned at the stake on May 30, 1431. She was nineteen years old.

Some thirty years later Joan was exonerated of all guilt, and she was ultimately canonized in 1920 by Pope Benedict XV, making official what the people had known for centuries.

> PRAYER: *Lord, You wondrously raised up St. Joan, Your Virgin, to defend the Faith and her country. Through her intercession grant that the Church may overcome the snares of her enemies and enjoy unbroken peace.*

~ Patroness of France ~

~ *Patron of Blacksmiths* ~

SAINT JOHN THE BAPTIST

June 24

THE feast of the Nativity, or birthday, of St. John the Baptist, the precursor of the Messiah and born six months before Him, is observed on June 24, and is one of the oldest feasts in the liturgy of the Church. He was the son of Zechariah and Elizabeth, a cousin of the Blessed Virgin Mary. Tradition places the home and birthplace of the Baptist near the village of Ain-Karim, six miles west of Jerusalem, where a Franciscan church marks the site. The church is called "St. John in the Mountains."

What we know of this Saint and great prophet, from his sanctification before his birth to his martyrdom under King Herod, is set down in Holy Scripture. He has always had a chief place in the veneration given by Holy Church to the heroic servants of God. While the feast of other Saints is celebrated on the day of their death, when their final victory is won, the birthday of St. John the Baptist is his feast day. We have also the feast of the Birth of Mary Immaculate.

Thirty years after the birth of Jesus, John began his mission on the banks of the Jordan. He was the last of the prophets of the Old Covenant. His work was to prepare the way and announce the coming of the long-expected Messiah, the Redeemer, in Whom all flesh would see "the salvation of God." He had the honor of baptizing his Divine Master and pointing Him out as "the Lamb of God Who takes away the sin of the world."

Shortly afterward, John rebuked Herod Antipas, the ruler in Galilee and Perea, for taking Herodias, the wife of the ruler's brother Philip. In retaliation, John was cast into prison and while there arranged—through his followers—to bear witness to Jesus one last time. John was then beheaded by order of Herod at the instigation of Herodias.

Before St. John was born, an Angel announced that "many would rejoice in his birth," and so June 24 is ranked among the joyous feasts of the year.

PRAYER: *God, You raised up St. John the Baptist to prepare a perfect people for Christ. Fill Your people with the joy of possessing Your grace and direct the minds of all the faithful in the way of peace and salvation.*

SAINT JOHN BOSCO

Priest

January 31

ST. JOHN BOSCO was born on a poor farm near Turin, Italy, in 1815. At an age when the modern child would be enjoying the pastime of a kindergarten education, he was out on the hillside tending sheep. At about his ninth year, when he expressed the desire to become a priest, it was found possible to let him commence his education by walking more than four miles daily for half a year. The other half, in spring and summer, was spent in the fields.

The day before he entered the seminary, his mother, laying her hands on his shoulders as he stood robed in his clerical dress, said: "To see you dressed in this manner fills my heart with joy. But remember that it is not the dress that gives honor to the state, but the practice of virtue. If at any time you come to doubt your vocation, I beseech you, lay it aside at once. I would rather have a poor peasant for my son than a negligent priest. When you came into the world I consecrated you to Our Lady; when you began to study I bade you honor her and

have recourse to her in all your difficulties; now I beg you to take her for your Queen."

Today the motto on the Salesian coat of arms: *Da mihi animas cetera tolle tibi*—"Give me only souls and keep all the rest"— bears witness to the fidelity of Don Bosco to the words of a truly Christian mother.

This admirable "Apostle of Youth" is almost our contemporary. He founded the Salesian Society of St. Francis de Sales and the Daughters of Mary Help of Christians. His life's work was consecrated to the care of young boys and girls.

St. John Bosco's success with youth flowed from his approach: showing them much love, imposing few restraints, manifesting true concern for their development, and giving them personal and religious encouragement. As his work expanded, he was able to cover the cost by preaching, writing popular books, and accepting charitable donations.

He died in 1888 and was canonized in 1934 by Pope Pius XI.

PRAYER: *God of mercy, You called St. John Bosco to be a father and teacher of the young. Grant that inspired by his ardent charity we may serve You alone and never tire of bringing others to Your Kingdom.*

~ *Patron of Editors* ~

~ Wholeheartedly Devoted to the Blessed Virgin ~

SAINT JOHN OF THE CROSS

Priest and Doctor of the Church

December 14

JOHN YEPEZ was born at Fontiberos in Old Castile, Spain, in 1542. From a very young age he evinced a great devotion toward the Blessed Virgin, of whose Order he became one of the brightest ornaments. After studying in a Jesuit college, he took the Carmelite habit, in the monastery of that Order at Medina del Campo in 1563, and practiced the greatest austerities. In 1567 he was ordained a priest.

Shortly after, he met St. Teresa of Avila at Medina del Campo, at which time she interested him in the work of reforming the Order. He entered heartily into her plans, and when the first monastery of Discalced Carmelite Friars was opened at Duruelo, John Yepez (who was to be St. John of the Cross) was its first member.

He successively filled the posts of superior, prior, vicar-general, and definitor. In the midst of his exterior labors his heart was always intimately united to God; he is known in the Church as one of the great contemplatives and teachers of mystical theology.

In his last illness he had a choice between two monasteries; one of them was a pleasant residence and its prior was his intimate friend, but he chose the other, the one of Ubeda, which was poor and where the prior was ill-disposed toward him. After much suffering, he died in 1591.

St. John has written some of the greatest spiritual classics of world literature. In the struggle between the Calced and Discalced Carmelites, he was briefly imprisoned at a house in Toledo by the former. It was then that he started to compose the first verses of his *Spiritual Canticle*.

Then in the years following his release he wrote *The Ascent of Mount Carmel*, *The Living Flame of Love*, and *The Dark Night of the Soul*. All of these books consist of poems followed by a long prose explanation setting forth the path to attain union with God.

St. John was beatified in 1675 by Pope Clement X, canonized in 1726 by Pope Benedict XIII, and declared a Doctor of the Church in 1926 by Pope Pius XI.

PRAYER: *God, Your Priest St. John became a model of perfect self-denial and showed us how to love the Cross. May we always imitate him and be rewarded with the eternal contemplation of Your glory.*

SAINT JOHN THE EVANGELIST

Apostle

December 27

ST. JOHN, the son of Zebedee, and the brother of St. James the Greater, was called to be an Apostle by our Lord in the first year of His public ministry. He was the youngest Apostle and the closest to Christ, and became known as the "beloved Apostle." Together with his brother, James "the Greater" and Peter, he was privileged to be present at the Transfiguration of the Lord, the healing of Peter's mother-in-law, the raising of the daughter of Jairus, and the Agony in the Garden.

It was John, together with Peter, whom Christ entrusted to prepare for the Passover, and it was John who at the Last Supper placed his head on the breast of Christ to learn the identity of the one who would betray Him. Then John was the only one of the Twelve who did not forsake the Savior in the hour of His Passion. He stood faithfully at the Cross, whence the Savior made him His Mother's guardian.

Together with Peter, John was the first to be at the tomb of the Risen Christ. After the Lord's Ascension, John was imprisoned briefly with Peter and appeared before the Sanhedrin with him, accompanied Peter to impart the Holy Spirit to the new converts in Samaria, and was present at the Council of Jerusalem in 49. Then he went to Ephesus in Asia Minor where he founded many churches and was doubtless present at Mary's death.

Tradition relates that the beloved disciple was brought to Rome and by order of Emperor Domitian cast into a caldron of boiling oil but came forth unharmed and was banished to the island of Patmos for a year, where he is thought to have written the Book of Revelation. After Domitian's death, he returned to Ephesus in 96 and wrote his Gospel and three Epistles. He died about the year 100.

St. John is known as the Apostle of Charity, a virtue that he had learned from his Divine Master and constantly inculcated by word and example. He is also called "the Divine" because of his theological depth, and he is often symbolized by an eagle because of the sublime heights to which his Gospel soars.

PRAYER: *God, through St. John the Apostle You willed to unlock to us the secrets of Your Word. Grant that what he has so excellently poured into our ears, we may properly understand.*

~ *Patron of Asia Minor* ~

~ Dedicated to American Missions ~

SAINT JOHN NEUMANN

Bishop

January 5

JOHN NEUMANN was born in Bohemia on March 28, 1811. Since he had a great desire to dedicate himself to the missions, he came to the United States as a cleric and was ordained in New York in 1836 by Bishop Dubois.

On January 16, 1842, he made his profession as a Redemptorist, the first to do so in America. He labored diligently in Ohio, Pennsylvania, and Maryland. In 1847, he was placed in charge of all the Redemptorists in America and became vice-provincial in 1848.

In this office, St. John stabilized the finances of individual Redemptorist houses and enhanced the schools of the order. He also published two catechisms and a Bible history in German. When his term of office was up, he served as a consultor. From 1851 to 1852 he was the rector of St. Alphonsus Church in Baltimore.

In March 1852, St. John was consecrated Bishop of Philadelphia. For the next eight years, he traveled throughout his diocese, encouraging priests and laity to work for the expansion of the Church in their area. He brought about the establishment of parish schools and the erection of many parishes.

He was responsible for the construction of some eighty new churches and saw the enrollment of children in parochial schools jump from five hundred to about ten thousand. He introduced eight new religious orders into the diocese. He also held three synods for priests and founded a new branch of the Sisters of the Third Order of St. Francis.

St. John was present at the first Plenary Council of Baltimore and two Provincial Councils and assisted at the proclamation of the dogma of the Immaculate Conception by Pope Pius IX at Rome in 1854.

Finally, he organized the first Catholic diocesan school board in America and was the first Bishop of the United States to prescribe the Forty Hours Devotion in his diocese. He died on January 5, 1860, and was canonized on June 19, 1977, by Pope Paul VI.

PRAYER: *God, You established St. John as Bishop in Your Church to feed Your flock by his word and form it by his example. Help us through his intercession to keep the Faith he taught by his word and follow the way he showed by his example.*

SAINT JOSEPH

Husband of Mary

March 19

ST. JOSEPH, the pure spouse of the Blessed Virgin Mary and foster-father of our Blessed Lord, was descended from the royal house of David. He is the "just man" of the New Testament, the lowly village carpenter of Nazareth, who among all men of the world was the one chosen by God to be the husband and protector of the Virgin Mother of Jesus Christ, God Incarnate. To his faithful, loving care was entrusted the childhood and youth of the Redeemer of the world.

After the Mother of God, not one of the children of men was ever so gifted and adorned with natural and supernatural virtues as was St. Joseph, her spouse. In purity of heart, in chastity of life, in humility, patience, fortitude, gentleness, and manliness of character, he reveals to us the perfect type and model of the true Christian.

Poor and obscure in this world's possessions and honors, he was rich in grace and merit, and eminent before God in the nobility and beauty of holiness. Because St. Joseph was the divinely appointed head of the Holy Family, which was the beginning of the great Family of God, the Church of Christ, on December 8, 1870, the Vicar of Jesus Christ, Pope Pius IX, solemnly proclaimed the foster-father of Jesus as Patron of the Universal Church, and from that time his feast has been celebrated on March 19 as one of high rank. In some places it is observed as a holy day of obligation.

Devotion to St. Joseph, fervent in the East from the early ages, has in later times spread and increased in such a marvelous way that in our day the Catholics of all nations vie with one another in honoring him. Besides the feast of March 19 there is the feast of St. Joseph the Worker, Spouse of the Blessed Virgin Mary (May 1), promulgated in 1955.

From his throne of glory in heaven, St. Joseph watches over and protects the Church militant, and no one who calls on him in need ever calls in vain. He is the model of a perfect Christian life and the patron of a happy death.

PRAYER: *Almighty God, You entrusted to the faithful care of Joseph the beginnings of the mysteries of the world's salvation. Through his intercession may Your Church always be faithful in her service so that Your designs will be fulfilled.*

~ *Patron of the Universal Church* ~

~ Patron of Desperate Cases ~

SAINT JUDE

Apostle

October 28

ST. JUDE, known as Thaddaeus, was a brother of St. James the Less, and a relative of our Savior.

It was Jude who asked the Lord at the Last Supper: "Why is it that You will reveal Yourself to us and not to the world?" He found it hard to understand how the Kingdom of God was to come about without the Messiah publicly disclosing His glory. This may indicate that he belonged to the Zealots, a group that was concerned with the establishment of God's Kingdom as an independent one on earth.

After Christ's Ascension, Jude labored with great zeal for the conversion of the Gentiles. For ten years he worked as a missionary in the whole of Mesopotamia. In 49, he returned to Jerusalem for the First Council. Later he joined another Apostle, Simon, in Libya, where they preached the Gospel.

Tradition says that these two Apostles suffered martyrdom at Suanis, a city of Persia, where they had labored as missionaries. St. Jude was beaten to death with a club; hence, he is represented with a club in hand. He is also represented wearing the image of Christ hanging from his neck. It stems from a legendary story that he was sent in the Lord's place to visit a nearby ruler (King Agbar) and effected a cure of his illness. St. Jude's body was brought to Rome, and his relics are venerated in St. Peter's Basilica.

St. Jude is known mainly as the Patron of Desperate Cases and as the writer of an Epistle of the New Testament. Written about 62–65, it denounces the heresies of the Simonians, Nicolaites, and Gnostics and warns Christians against the seduction of false teaching.

To the pride of the wicked, Jude opposes the humble loyalty of the Archangel Michael. He encourages Christians to build a spiritual edifice by living lives founded upon faith, love of God, hope, and prayer. He stresses love of neighbor and urges all to convert non-Christians by their virtuous lives.

St. Jude concludes the Epistle with a prayer praising God for the Incarnation, by means of which the eternal Son of God, Jesus Christ, took upon Himself our human nature and redeemed mankind.

PRAYER: *God, You made Your Name known to us through the Apostles. By the intercession of St. Jude, let Your Church continue to grow with an increased number of believers.*

SAINT LOUISE DE MARILLAC

Religious

ST. LOUISE DE MARILLAC was born on August 15, 1591. In 1613 she married Antoine Le Gras, who died thirteen years later, leaving Louise with a young son.

Louise took a vow of widowhood and asked St. Vincent de Paul to be her spiritual director. This holy man, who was then known as Monsieur Vincent, counseled Louise for five years before allowing her to take part in caring for the poor and in visiting the Confraternities of Charity that he had founded.

In 1633, Louise's home became the quarters for the first candidates enrolled for the service of the sick and the poor. This was the beginning of the Daughters of Charity, Servants of the Sick Poor, dedicated to corporal and spiritual service of the poor in their homes.

In 1634, Louise, at her confessor's bidding, drafted a rule of life for the new Congregation, which took shape slowly. Finally, in 1642 four members were allowed to take annual vows of poverty, chastity, and obedience by St. Vincent.

In 1655, the Congregation received formal Roman approval and was placed under the direction of St. Vincent's own Congregation of Priests. With St. Louise leading the way, the Sisters cared for all the patients of the Paris Hospital called "God's Hotel." They also worked in a home for foundlings that St. Vincent had begun, both caring for the children and teaching them.

In their work together, St. Vincent found Louise de Marillac to be a woman of clear mind as well as great courage. She also showed an incredible amount of self-sacrifice in the face of her own ill health. Louise ever demonstrated humility and motherly care in her work with the poor and with her own Sisters.

At the same time, Louise never forgot her son and always prayed for his spiritual welfare. On her deathbed, she rejoiced to see him with his wife and child and gave them her blessing.

St. Louise died on March 15, 1660, six months before the death of St. Vincent himself. She was canonized in 1934 by Pope Pius X, and on February 10, 1960, Pope John XXIII proclaimed her Patroness of all Christian Social Workers.

PRAYER: *Lord, strengthen us through the intercession of St. Louise that we may advance rejoicing in the way of love.*

~ Patroness of Social Workers ~

~ *Patroness of the Blind* ~

SAINT LUCY

Virgin and Martyr

December 13

ST. LUCY, a native of Syracuse in Sicily, was from her cradle educated in the Faith of Christ under the care of her widowed mother, Eutychia. At an early age she made a vow of virginity.

Unaware of the vow, Eutychia pressed her daughter to marry a young gentleman who was not a Christian. While Lucy was able to forestall such a prospect from taking place, Eutychia became afflicted with discharges of blood. Lucy persuaded her mother to go with her to the tomb of St. Agatha at Catania and offer prayers for relief from her ailment. They did so and their prayers were answered.

Lucy then told her mother of her desire to devote herself to God in perpetual virginity and to give her fortune to the poor. In gratitude, Eutychia left her daughter at liberty to do what she wished.

Learning of Lucy's decision, the suitor became enraged and brought accusation against Lucy that she was a Christian. Since the persecution of the Emperor Diocletian was in full force, Lucy was haled into court. When she remained resolute in her faith, the judge ordered her to be exposed to prostitution in a brothel. However, with God's help Lucy was made unmovable so that the guards were unable to carry her to the brothel. She was also able to overcome fire and other torments used by her persecutors. Finally, after a long and glorious combat, Lucy achieved martyrdom through death by a sword about the year 304.

The Acts that tell the above story are regarded as unhistorical, but Lucy's connection with Syracuse and her early cult in the Church are unquestionable. She was honored at Rome in the sixth century, and her name was inserted in the Canon of the Mass (i.e., Eucharistic Prayer I), where it still remains.

During the Middle Ages St. Lucy was invoked by those who were afflicted with troubles of the eyes—possibly because her name means light or lucidity. As a result, various legends grew up that her eyes were plucked out and then restored to her, more beautiful than before.

> PRAYER: *Lord, may the intercession of Your Virgin and Martyr St. Lucy help us so that, as we celebrate her heavenly birthday on earth, we may contemplate her triumph in heaven.*

SAINT LUKE THE EVANGELIST

Evangelist

October 18

ST. LUKE was born at Antioch, Syria, according to the Church historian Eusebius. He was a Gentile by birth and a physician by profession. According to a legend of the sixth century he was also a painter.

He was one of the earliest converts to the Faith and later became the missionary companion of St. Paul, whom he accompanied on part of his second and third missionary journeys, and attended during his Caesarean and Roman captivities. Little is known with certainty of his subsequent life.

The unanimous tradition of the Church ascribes the third Gospel to St. Luke. Allusions to and citations from the Gospel are most frequent in early Christian writings, and even heretics made diligent use of this inspired book. The Gospel itself shows that its author was a person of literary powers, a physician, and a companion of St. Paul. Early Christian tradition ascribes the Gospel and its companion volume, The Acts of the Apostles, to approximately 75 A.D.

Little is known with certainty about the place of composition. Some of the ancient authors suggest Achaia (Greece); some of the manuscripts mention Alexandria or Macedonia; while modern writers also defend Caesarea, Ephesus, or Rome.

Luke portrays Christianity as a religious faith open to all people. His portrait of Jesus identifies Him as the expected Messiah, Who is the Son of God and Son of Man, and manifests the Savior's concern for humanity and His identification with the poor, the outcast, and the criminal. He also gives prominence to Christ's teaching on prayer and to the women who followed him as well as to women in general.

Luke is represented in art by an ox, the animal of sacrifice, because he begins his Gospel with the story of Zechariah the priest offering sacrifice to God.

PRAYER: *God, You chose St. Luke to reveal in preaching and writing Your love for the poor. Grant that those who already glory in Your Name may persevere in one heart and one mind, and that all people may hear Your Good News of salvation.*

~ *Patron of Doctors and Painters* ~

~ Patroness of Youth ~

SAINT MARIA GORETTI

Virgin and Martyr

July 6

ST. MARIA GORETTI, called by Pope Pius XII "the St. Agnes of the twentieth century," was born on a small farm near Ancona, Italy, in 1890. The third of seven children, she was, according to her mother, happy, good, openhearted, never disobedient, without whim, and had a sense and seriousness beyond her years. Her father died when she was nine, and Maria helped out with the younger children and the housework while her mother ran the farm.

She received First Communion at eleven. Six months later, she was severely tried for her Faith. The Goretti family shared a home with the partner of their father and his son, Alexander, a wicked-minded youth who began making sinful advances toward Maria. She repelled them immediately but said nothing about them for he threatened to kill her and her mother if she did. Finally, lust drove Alexander to attack outright, but again the Saint resisted him, crying out repeatedly: "No, it's a sin! God does not want it!" Overwhelmed by fear and anger, Alexander began to strike at her blindly with a long dagger, landing several vicious blows to her body.

St. Maria was rushed to the hospital at Nettuno, but it soon became evident that nothing could be done. Before receiving Communion the next morning, she was asked about her attitude toward Alexander. She replied clearly that she forgave him, that she would pray for his repentance, and that she wished to see him in heaven. On July 6, 1902, this saintly maiden died and went to meet her heavenly Spouse for Whose love she had been willing to give her life. Years later her attacker repented, left prison, and became a Capuchin lay brother.

On July 25, 1950, Maria was raised to sainthood by Pope Pius XII, with her mother, brothers, and sisters present, a unique event in the history of the Church.

PRAYER: *God, Author of innocence and Lover of chastity, You conferred on St. Maria the grace of martyrdom at a youthful age. Through her intercession grant us constancy in Your Commandments, You Who gave the crown to a virgin who fought for You.*

SAINT MARIA SOLEDAD TORRES-ACOSTA

Religious

EMANUELA TORRES-ACOSTA was born on December 2, 1826, at Madrid, Spain. From her earliest days, she felt called to the service of God as a vowed religious. She applied to enter the Dominican Order but was rejected because of poor health.

Emanuela learned that Father Michael Martinez was starting a new congregation of young women that would provide nurses to visit the homes of the sick poor who could not go to hospitals. So she asked to join the new group. When the priest saw how small and frail Emanuela was, he accepted her only with reservations. Little did he imagine that she would be the only one of the original seven to withstand the rigors and hardships of the early days of the foundation.

Emanuela took the habit in 1851, at the age of twenty-four, and changed her name to Maria Soledad. She gave herself wholeheartedly to serving God through the sick. She visited the mansions of the wealthy and the shanties of the poor—always bringing God's love together with her nursing skills. She triumphed over her initial revulsion on viewing the diseased bodies by seeing Christ in each person.

Maria oversaw the beginnings of the community, which experienced significant internal discord and split into two groups in 1855.

Half of the sisters remained with Maria Soledad, and under the direction of a new moderator, Father Gabino Sanchez, a new community was formed. It was named Handmaids of Mary Serving the Sick. It received diocesan approbation in 1861, and Maria Soledad was recognized as the superioress, a position she held for the next thirty-five years.

The Handmaids of Mary received tremendous public acclaim for their heroic work during the Madrid cholera epidemic of 1865. The community also expanded throughout Europe and the Americas. After founding forty-six houses, Maria Soledad died on October 11, 1887. She was raised to Sainthood by Pope Paul VI in 1970.

> PRAYER: *Lord God, Your Son showed us His deep care for the poor. Through the intercession of St. Maria Soledad, may we cultivate a loving concern for the poor both in prayer and in works.*

~ Handmaid of Mary Serving the Sick ~

PAX
TIBI
MAR
CE

EVAN
GELIS
TA
MEVS

~ Patron of Notaries ~

SAINT MARK THE EVANGELIST
April 25

THE second Gospel was written by St. Mark, who, in the New Testament, is sometimes called John Mark. Both he and his mother, Mary, were highly esteemed in the early Church, and his mother's house in Jerusalem served as a meeting place for Christians there.

St. Mark was associated with St. Paul and St. Barnabas (who was Mark's cousin) on their missionary journey through the island of Cyprus. Later he accompanied St. Barnabas alone. We know also that he was in Rome with St. Peter and with St. Paul. Tradition ascribes to him the founding of the Church in Alexandria.

St. Mark wrote the second Gospel, probably in Rome sometime before the year 60 A.D.; he wrote it in Greek for the Gentile converts to Christianity. Tradition tells us that St. Mark was requested by the Romans to set down the teachings of St. Peter. This seems to be confirmed by the position that St. Peter has in this Gospel. In this way the second Gospel is a record of the life of Jesus as seen through the eyes of the Prince of the Apostles.

This Gospel is short, vivid, concrete, and gives the impression of immediate contact with Jesus. It makes use of a familiar style that is occasionally awkward but always direct, and might almost be called photographic in its handling of details.

Mark desires to establish a close bond between the Passion of Jesus and His Lordship, showing that the Son of Man had to endure the Cross before attaining His glory and that His destiny is one of the Suffering Servant prophesied by Isaiah. It is also Mark's design to teach us that if we want to encounter the living Christ, we must follow His Way.

Mark is represented in art by a lion because he begins his Gospel with St. John the Baptist, "the voice of one crying out in the wilderness."

PRAYER: *God our Father, You helped St. Mark the Evangelist with Your grace so that he could preach the Good News of Christ. Help us to know You well so that we may faithfully live our lives as followers of Christ.*

SAINT MARTIN DE PORRES

Religious

ST. MARTIN DE PORRES was born at Lima, Peru, in 1579. His father was a Spanish gentleman and his mother an Indian woman from Panama. At fifteen, he became a lay brother at the Dominican Friary at Lima and spent his whole life there—as a barber, farm-laborer, almoner, and infirmarian among other things.

Martin had a great desire to go off to some foreign mission and thus earn the palm of martyrdom. However, since this was not possible, he made a martyr out of his body, devoting himself to ceaseless and severe penances. In turn, God endowed him with many graces and wondrous gifts, such as aerial flights and bilocation.

Martin's care for the sick extended to all the people of the city, and he succeeded in establishing an orphanage and a foundling hospital there. He was placed in charge of distributing daily alms of food to the poor, and he is said to have increased it miraculously at times. He also cared for the slaves who were brought to Peru from Africa.

St. Martin's love was all-embracing, shown equally to humans and animals, including vermin, and he maintained a cats' and dogs' hospital at his sister's house. He also possessed spiritual wisdom, demonstrated in his solving his sister's marriage problems, raising a dowry for his niece inside of three days' time, and resolving theological problems for the learned of his Order and for Bishops.

Martin loved to fast and to pray—above all to pray at night after the example of Jesus. In prayer he obtained great enlightenment, which gave a wonderful flavor to his catechetical lessons. His whole life, hidden and radiant at the same time, unfolded in a world filled with Angels and demons, in which Martin always preserved a perfect serenity.

A close friend of St. Rose of Lima, this saintly man died on November 3, 1639, and was canonized in 1962 by Pope John XXIII.

PRAYER: *God, You led St. Martin by the way of humility to heavenly glory. Help us to follow the example of his holiness and so become worthy to be exalted with him in heaven.*

~ Patron of Hairdressers and of Social Justice ~

~ Patroness of Provence ~

SAINT MARY MAGDALENE

July 22

ST. MARY, whom Jesus converted, and who witnessed His last moments with Mary His Mother and St. John, was called Magdalene from the town of Magdala in Galilee. Clement of Alexandria and others identify her with the woman who washed Jesus' feet with her tears. Others regard her as Mary, the sister of Martha and Lazarus. She followed Jesus with other devout women during His public life.

In the darkest hour of her Lord's life, Mary stood at some distance, watching Him on the Cross. Then with "the other Mary" she saw the great stone rolled before the door of the tomb in which the Lord's body was placed. It was also Mary who, weeping by the sepulcher early on the first day of the week, was the first to see the Risen Lord—the first witness to the Resurrection without which our faith is vain.

Jesus said to her, "Woman, why are you weeping? Whom are you looking for?" Thinking He was the gardener, she said to Him, "Sir, if you have removed Him, tell me where you have put Him, and I will take Him away." Jesus said to her, "Mary!" She turned and said to Him "Teacher."

Jesus then said to her, "Do not hold on to Me, because I have not yet ascended to My Father. But go to My brothers and tell them, 'I am ascending to My Father and your Father, to my God and your God.'" Mary went and announced to the disciples, "I have seen the Lord," and revealed what He had said.

It is an ancient tradition in Provence, France, that St. Mary Magdalene or Mary the sister of Lazarus, together with Lazarus, Martha, and some other disciples of our Lord, put to sea and landed at Marseilles; and that St. Lazarus became the first Bishop of that See.

The feast of St. Mary Magdalene is celebrated by the Greeks as well as the Latins on this date. However, in the instructions given with the latest edition of the Roman Calendar, the Latin Church has stipulated that the feast is solely that of the woman to whom Christ appeared and not that of the sister of Lazarus or the penitent woman.

PRAYER: *God, it was to St. Mary Magdalene before all others that Your Son committed the message of Easter joy. Through her intercession may we one day contemplate Him reigning in glory.*

SAINT MATTHEW THE EVANGELIST

Apostle

September 21

ST. MATTHEW, one of the twelve Apostles, is the author of the first Gospel. This has been the constant tradition of the Church and is confirmed by the Gospel itself. The son of Alpheus, he was called to be an Apostle while sitting in the tax collector's place at Capernaum. He is identified with the "Levi" of Mark and Luke.

His apostolic activity was at first restricted to the communities of Palestine. Nothing definite is known about his later life. There is a tradition that points to Ethiopia as his field of labor; other traditions make mention of Parthia and Persia. It is uncertain whether he died naturally or was martyred.

St. Matthew's Gospel was written to fill a sorely-felt want for both believers and unbelievers. For the former, it served as a token of his regard and as an encouragement in the trial to come; for the latter, it was designed to convince them that the Messiah had come in the Person of Jesus, our Lord, in Whom all the promises of the Messianic Kingdom embracing all people had been fulfilled in a spiritual rather than in a carnal way: "My Kingdom is not of this world."

Writing for his countrymen of Palestine, St. Matthew composed his Gospel in his native Aramaic, the "Hebrew tongue" mentioned in the Gospel and the Acts of the Apostles. Soon afterward, about the time of the persecution of Herod Agrippa I in 42 A.D., he left for other lands. Another tradition places the composition of his Gospel either between the time of this departure and the Council of Jerusalem in 49 A.D., or even later.

Definitely, however, the Gospel itself, depicting the Holy City with its altar and temple as still existing, and without any reference to the fulfillment of our Lord's prophecy, shows that it was written before the destruction of the city by the Romans (70 A.D.), and this internal evidence confirms the early traditions.

St. Matthew is represented in art by a man because he begins his Gospel with Christ's earthly ancestry and stresses his human and kingly character.

PRAYER: *God, You chose St. Matthew the Publican to become an Apostle. By following his example and benefiting by his prayers, may we always follow and abide by Your will.*

~ *Patron of Bankers* ~

~ Patron of Prisoners ~

— 124 —

SAINT MAXIMILIAN KOLBE

Priest and Martyr

August 14

MAXIMILIAN was born in 1894 in Poland and became a Franciscan. He contracted tuberculosis and, though he recovered, he remained frail all his life. Before his ordination as a priest, Maximilian founded the Immaculata Movement devoted to our Lady. After receiving a doctorate in theology, he spread the Movement through a magazine entitled "The Knight of the Immaculata" and helped form a community of eight hundred men.

Maximilian went to Japan where he built a comparable monastery and then on to India where he furthered the Movement. In 1936 he returned home because of ill health. After the Nazi invasion in 1939, he was imprisoned and released for a time. But in 1941 he was arrested again and sent to the concentration camp at Auschwitz.

On July 31, 1941, in reprisal for one prisoner's escape, ten men were chosen to die. Father Kolbe offered himself in place of a husband and father and was the last to die, enduring two weeks of starvation, thirst, and neglect. He was canonized in 1981 by Pope John Paul II.

Present at the canonization was Francis Gajowniczec, the man whose life Father Kolbe saved. In a later interview, he said: "I was standing in the same row as Father Kolbe, four or five places away. . . . I had heard others speak about him as a priest who brought new courage to the despairing and gave them some of his bread.

"The camp commandant . . . approached me and pointed his finger. I couldn't refrain from crying out: 'My God! My wife and my children!' But I joined the other condemned men. At that point, a prisoner, number 16670, came out of his row and spoke. . . .

" 'I ask to take the place of this man.' 'Which one?' asked the commandant. 'This head of a family. I have no wife and children. I am a Catholic priest.' . . . [He had] a firm look and an assured voice. When he took my place, I went back to my spot. We did not exchange a word—just a glance."

PRAYER: *Lord, You inflamed St. Maximilian with love for the Virgin Mary and filled him with zeal for souls and love for neighbor. Through his prayers, enable us to work for Your glory in serving others and so be conformed to Your Son until death.*

SAINT MICHAEL

Archangel

September 29

ANGELS are spirits without bodies, who possess superior intelligence, gigantic strength, and surpassing holiness. They enjoy an intimate relationship to God as His special adopted children, contemplating, loving, and praising Him in heaven. Some of them are frequently sent to earth as messengers from on high.

In her Liturgy the Church honors three Angels who were sent by God to man over the course of the ages: Michael, Gabriel, and Raphael. They are termed Archangels, the second of nine choirs of Angels, which are in descending order: Seraphim, Cherubim, Thrones, Dominations, Virtues, Powers, Principalities, Archangels, and Angels.

St. Michael has always been regarded as the protector of Christians against the devil, especially at the hour of death when he conducts the soul to God.

Devotion to him apparently started in Phrygia and soon spread to the West on the strength of the legend that he appeared at Mount Garganus in northern Italy during the pontificate of Pope Gelasius (492–496) and pointed out a spot on which a shrine in his honor was to be established.

St. Michael is usually represented with a sword and battling with a conquered dragon. From the sixth century on, his feast was celebrated alone on September 29, which was known as Michaelmas Day in some parts. In 1970, his feast was joined with the feasts of Sts. Gabriel and Raphael.

The name Michael signifies "Who is like to God?" and was the war cry of the good Angels in the battle fought in heaven against Satan and his followers. Holy Scripture describes St. Michael as "one of the chief princes," and as leader of the forces of heaven in their triumph over the powers of hell. He has been especially honored and invoked as patron and protector by the Church from the time of the Apostles. Although he is always called "the Archangel," the Greek Fathers and many others place him over all the Angels—as Prince of the Seraphim.

PRAYER: *God, with great wisdom You direct the ministry of Angels and people. Grant that those who always minister to You in heaven may defend us during our life on earth.*

~ Patron of Police Officers~

~ Patron of Bakers and Pawnbrokers ~

SAINT NICHOLAS

Bishop

December 6

IT is the common opinion that St. Nicholas was a native of Patara in Lycia, Asia Minor. He became a monk in the monastery of Holy Zion near Myra. Of this house he was made Abbot by the Archbishop, its founder. When the See of Myra, the capital of Lycia, fell vacant, St. Nicholas was appointed its Archbishop. It is said that he suffered for the Faith under Diocletian, and that he was present at the Council of Nicea as an opponent of Arianism. His death occurred at Myra, in the year 342.

The characteristic virtue of St. Nicholas appears to have been his charity for the poor. It is also related that he was mortified and abstemious from a very young age.

There is a legendary story of three girls whose father was about to turn them into prostitutes because he did not have enough money to give them a dowry at marriage time. Nicholas learned of their situation, and on three different occasions tossed bags of gold into their house. Thus, the girls were married with dignity and avoided their poor father's desperate plan for them.

This led to the practice of children giving presents at Christmas in the Saint's name. In turn the name St. Nicholas was transformed into Sint Klaes by the Dutch and ultimately became Santa Claus.

The Emperor Justinian built a church in honor of St. Nicholas at Constantinople in the suburb of Blacharnae, about the year 340. Then the Saint gained even greater popularity when his relics were brought to Bari, Italy, in 1087, and his shrine became one of the greatest centers of pilgrimage in the Middle Ages. Indeed, it is said that St. Nicholas has been represented in Christian art more frequently than any other Saint except our Lady.

He has always been honored with great veneration in the Latin and Greek Churches. The Russian Church seems to honor him more than any other Saint after the Apostles.

PRAYER: *We call upon Your mercy, O Lord. Through the intercession of St. Nicholas, keep us safe amid all dangers so that we may go forward without hindrance on the road of salvation.*

SAINT PATRICK
Bishop and Apostle of Ireland
March 17

THE date and place of St. Patrick's birth are uncertain. He was born about the year 389, the son of Calpurnius, a Roman-British deacon, and Conchessa. When he was sixteen, he was carried as a captive into Ireland and obliged to serve a heathen master as a herdsman. Despite the harshness of the life there, he not only held on to his Faith but also learned the science of prayer and contemplation.

After six years he effected a miraculous escape and returned home. In a dream, he was told to go back and Christianize Ireland. St. Patrick prepared for his task by studying in the monastery of Lerins from about 412–415 and was ordained at Auxerre by St. Amator about 417.

In 431, after a period during which his vocation to Ireland was tested by the hesitancy of his superiors in entrusting such a mission to him, St. Patrick was sent to assist Bishop Paladius in Ireland. On the death of the latter, St. Patrick was consecrated Bishop by St. Germanus (432) after receiving the approbation of Pope Celestine I. He traveled the length and breadth of Ireland, planting the Faith everywhere despite the hostility of the Druids, and succeeded in converting several members of the royal family.

On a visit to Rome in 442, he was commissioned by Pope Leo the Great to organize the Church of Ireland and on his return made Armagh the primatial See, establishing Bishops in various places.

In winning a pagan nation for Christ, St. Patrick established many monasteries for men and women and made it famous for its seats of piety and learning. In the ensuing centuries Irish monks carried the Faith to England, France, and Switzerland.

After living a completely apostolic life of labor and prayer, St. Patrick died on March 17, 461, in the monastery of Saul, in Down in Ulster, leaving behind his *Confessions*, which give a vivid picture of a great man of God.

> PRAYER: *God, You sent Patrick to preach Your glory to the Irish people. Through his merits and intercession, grant that we who have the honor of bearing the name of Christian may constantly proclaim Your wonderful designs to others.*

~ *Patron of Ireland* ~

~ Patron of Public Relations ~

SAINT PAUL THE APOSTLE

June 29

ST. PAUL, the indefatigable Apostle of the Gentiles, was converted from Judaism on the road to Damascus.

He remained there some days after his Baptism, and then went to Arabia, possibly for a year or two, to prepare himself for his future missionary activity. Having returned to Damascus, he stayed there for a time, preaching in the synagogues that Jesus is the Christ, the Son of God. For this he incurred the anger of some Jews and had to flee from the city. He then went to Jerusalem to see Peter and pay his homage to the head of the Church.

Later he went back to his native Tarsus (Acts 9:30), evangelizing his own province until called by Barnabas to Antioch. After one year, both Barnabas and Paul were sent with alms to the poor Christian community at Jerusalem. Having fulfilled their mission, they returned to Antioch.

Soon after this Paul and Barnabas made the first missionary journey (44/45–49/50), visiting the island of Cyprus and locations in Asia Minor, and establishing churches at Pisidian Antioch, Iconium, Lystra, and Derbe.

After the Apostolic Council of Jerusalem Paul, accompanied by Silas and later also by Timothy and Luke, made his second missionary journey (50–52/53). First he revisited the churches he previously established in Asia Minor and then passed through Galatia. At Troas Paul had a vision of a Macedonian, which impressed him as a call from God to evangelize Macedonia. He accordingly sailed for Europe and preached the Gospel in Philippi, Thessalonica, Beroea, Athens, and Corinth. Then he returned to Antioch by way of Ephesus and Jerusalem.

On his third missionary journey (53/54–58) Paul visited nearly the same regions as on the second, but made Ephesus the center of his missionary activity. He laid plans also for another missionary journey, intending to leave Jerusalem for Rome and Spain. But persecutions hindered him from doing so. After two years of imprisonment at Caesarea he finally reached Rome, where he was kept another two years in chains.

During a second imprisonment in Rome, Paul was beheaded in 67.

PRAYER: *God, You give us a holy joy as we celebrate St. Paul. Grant that Your Church may follow his teaching and example in all things.*

SAINT PAUL OF THE CROSS

Priest

October 20

ST. PAUL OF THE CROSS was born at Ovada in the Republic of Genoa, January 3, 1694. His infancy and youth were spent in great innocence and piety. He formed a society among the youths of his neighborhood and was imitated in his mortifications by his younger brother John Baptist. In 1714, Paul answered a plea by Pope Clement XI for volunteers to fight against the Turks. However, after a year he was convinced that the army was not his vocation and obtained his discharge. Returning home, he resumed his life of prayer and penance.

In the summer of 1720, he was inspired from on high by a vision of our Lady to found a congregation; he beheld the habit that he and his companions were to wear. After consulting his director, Bishop Gastinara of Alexandria in Piedmont, he reached the conclusion that God wished him to establish a congregation in honor of the Passion of Jesus Christ.

On November 22, 1720, the Bishop vested him with the habit that had been shown to him in a vision. From that moment the Saint applied himself to prepare the Rules of his institute; and in 1721 he went to Rome with his brother to obtain the approbation of the Holy See. At first he failed, but he finally succeeded when Benedict XIV approved the Rules in 1741 and 1746. Meanwhile St. Paul built his first monastery near Obitello. Some time later the Saint established a larger community at the Church of Sts. John and Paul in Rome.

The principal purpose of the Congregation is to meditate on and proclaim the Passion and Death of the Lord. For the same purpose he also founded the Passionist Nuns as a contemplative community. He is considered the greatest mystic of the eighteenth century.

For fifty years St. Paul remained the indefatigable missionary of Italy. God lavished upon him the greatest gifts in the supernatural order, but he treated himself with the strictest rigor, and believed that he was a useless servant and a great sinner. His saintly death occurred at Rome in the year 1775, at the age of eighty-one. He was canonized in 1867 by Pope Pius IX.

PRAYER: *Lord, may the prayers of St. Paul who loved the Cross with a singular love gain Your grace for us. May we be inspired by his example and embrace our own cross with courage.*

~ Founder of the Passionist Congregation ~

~ *Patron of Fishermen and Watchmakers* ~

SAINT PETER THE APOSTLE

Apostle

June 29

ST. PETER was a fisherman of Galilee, named Simon, and the son of John. His brother Andrew introduced him to Christ about Whom they had probably heard from John the Baptist, and he became His disciple, ultimately giving up his family and possessions to follow Him. Christ changed his name to Peter (Rock) and made him the Rock on which His Church was to be built. After His Resurrection, Jesus conferred the primacy on Peter, and he became the Vicar of Christ and the head of the Apostles, the first Pope.

The Gospels speak about Peter more than any other Apostle. He often was honored; several miracles were performed for his benefit; Christ stayed at his home, preached from his boat, sent him the first message of the Resurrection, and appeared to him personally. Often Peter acted as spokesman for the other Apostles. Finally, mention is made of his defects: his anger, imperfect faith, impetuosity, and his triple denial of Christ.

After the Ascension Peter began his work as head of the Church. He directed the election of Matthias, delivered the first public Apostolic sermon, cured a man lame from birth, and received a Divine commission to receive Gentiles into the Church. After the execution of James, the brother of John, by Herod Agrippa, Peter was miraculously rescued from prison. He presided at the Apostolic Council of Jerusalem in the year 49, when it was officially declared that the Gentile converts to the Faith were not subject to the Jewish law of circumcision. Afterward, he went to Antioch, where it was decided that Christians were not bound to observe the Mosaic Law.

St. Peter dwelt in Rome intermittently for twenty-five years as founder and first Bishop of the Church there. Finally, in the last year of Nero's reign, 67, he was crucified with his head downward, at his own request, not deeming himself worthy to die as did his Divine Master. Two Epistles of the New Testament are attributed to him, and the Gospel of St. Mark, who was his disciple, has been called "The Gospel of Peter."

PRAYER: *God, You give us a holy joy as we celebrate St. Peter. Grant that Your Church may always follow his teaching and example.*

SAINT PETER CANISIUS

Priest and Doctor of the Church

THIS eminent Jesuit was born in Nijmegen, Holland (when it was part of Germany), May 8, 1521. At twenty-two years of age he joined the Society of Jesus and distinguished himself in studies and spiritual perfection. He was the second great Apostle of Germany, as well as a preacher, theologian, and leader of the Counter-Reformation.

His apostolate became preaching and the founding of Jesuit institutions of higher learning. He attended the Council of Trent as the theologian for the Bishop of Augsburg and spoke twice, at the sessions in Trent and in Bologna.

He helped to settle a dispute between the Emperor and Pope Pius IV and was chosen to promulgate the decrees of the Council of Trent in Germany. In 1580, he founded a college at Fribourg that became the University of Fribourg —and remained Catholic thanks to his preaching.

St. Peter wrote and published a great deal, and he is regarded as one of the creators of a Catholic press. Among other things, he edited the works of St. Cyril of Alexandria and St. Leo the Great, an edition of St. Jerome's letters, a Martyrology, a revision of the Breviary, and a *Manual of Catholics*.

With astonishing clarity this devout man of God saw that in order to combat the Reformation the Church must first reform herself in her pastors and prepare generations of instructed laymen capable of defending their Faith. Of the many works that flowed from his pen, the most celebrated remains a Catechism, which appeared in 1560 and went on to achieve two hundred editions before the turn of the century. Entitled *Summary of Christian Doctrine*, it was followed by two shorter catechisms. All three were used effectively in schools during the Catholic Reformation.

He died at Fribourg, Switzerland, in 1597. Pope Pius XI canonized him on May 21, 1925, and named him a Doctor of the Church.

PRAYER: *God, You gave St. Peter Canisius wisdom and courage to defend the Catholic Faith. Through his intercession, grant that those who seek the truth may joyfully find You and that believers may ever persevere in bearing witness to You.*

~ *Founder of Numerous Jesuit Colleges* ~

~ *Patron of the Black Missions* ~

SAINT PETER CLAVER

Priest

September 9

ST. PETER CLAVER was born at Verdu, Catalonia, Spain, in 1580, of impoverished parents descended from ancient and distinguished families. He studied at the Jesuit College of Barcelona, entered the Jesuit novitiate at Tarragona in 1602, and took his final vows on August 8, 1604. While studying philosophy at Majorca, the young religious was influenced by St. Alphonsus Rodriguez to go to the Indies and save "millions of those perishing souls."

In 1610, he landed at Cartagena (modern Colombia), the principal slave market of the New World, where a thousand slaves were brought every month. After his ordination in 1615, he dedicated himself to the service of the Black slaves—a work that was to last for thirty-three years. He labored unceasingly for the salvation of the slaves and the abolition of the slave trade, and the love he lavished on them was something that transcended the natural order.

Boarding the slave ships as they entered the harbor, he would hurry to the revolting inferno of the hold, and offer whatever poor refreshments he could afford; he would care for the sick and dying, and instruct the slaves through Black catechists, before administering the Sacraments. Through his efforts three hundred thousand souls entered the Church. Furthermore, he did not lose sight of his converts when they left the ships, but followed them to the plantations to which they were sent, encouraged them to live as Christians, and prevailed on their masters to treat them humanely.

The Saint also ministered to the lepers in St. Lazarus Hospital and to condemned prisoners and was always available for confessions. He preached in the city's main square, conducted missions with great success, and led an austere and holy life. He died in 1654 and was canonized in 1888 by Pope Leo XIII.

PRAYER: *God, You conferred on St. Peter Claver love and patience to help Your enslaved people and bring them to a knowledge of Your Name. Through his intercession, help us to seek equality for all races.*

SAINTS PHILIP AND JAMES
Apostles
May 3

ST. PHILIP, a native of Beth-saida in Galilee, was called by our Lord the day after St. Peter and St. Andrew. We learn from tradition that he was then a married man, and that he had several daughters, three of whom reached eminent sanctity. Like the other Apostles, St. Philip left all things to follow Christ. His name is frequently mentioned in the Holy Gospels.

After the Ascension of his Divine Master, St. Philip preached the Gospel in that part of Asia Minor called Phrygia, which was then a province of the Roman Empire. It is supposed that he was buried at Hierapolis in Phrygia.

ST. JAMES THE LESS, the author of the first Catholic Epistle, was the son of Alphaeus (also known as Cleophas). His mother Mary was either a sister or a close relative of the Blessed Virgin, and for that reason, according to Jewish custom, he was sometimes called the brother of the Lord. The Apostle held a distinguished position in the early Christian community of Jerusalem. St. Paul tells us he was a witness of the Resurrection of Christ; he is also called a "pillar" of the Church, whom St. Paul consulted about the Gospel.

According to tradition, he was the first Bishop of Jerusalem, and was at the Council of Jerusalem about the year 49. The historians Eusebius and Hegesippus relate that St. James was martyred for the Faith in the Spring of the year 62, although they greatly esteemed his person and had given him the surname of "James the Just."

Tradition has always recognized him as the author of the Epistle that bears his name. Internal evidence based on the language, style, and teaching of the Epistle reveals its author as a Jew familiar with the Old Testament, and a Christian thoroughly grounded in the teachings of the Gospel. External evidence from the early Fathers and Councils of the Church confirms its authenticity and canonicity. The burden of his discourse is an exhortation to practical Christian living.

PRAYER: *Lord God, we enjoy celebrating the annual feast of Your Apostles Sts. Philip and James. Through their prayers let us share in the Passion and the Resurrection of Your Son and help us merit Your eternal presence.*

~ *(St. James) Patron of Hatmakers* ~

~ *Patron of Rome* ~

SAINT PHILIP NERI

Priest

May 26

ST. PHILIP was born in Florence in 1515, the very same year that St. Teresa was born at Avila in Spain. From his sixth year he was characterized by the most perfect obedience toward his parents. Having finished his classical studies at eighteen, he was sent to an uncle who lived near Monte Cassino. But St. Philip, desirous of serving God without worldly distractions, went to Rome in 1533 and became preceptor to the children of a Florentine nobleman.

Even at this period of his life he obtained a great reputation for sanctity. While teaching others he devoted himself to the study of philosophy and theology. His desire to save souls caused him to establish the Confraternity of the Blessed Trinity in 1548, with the object of serving pilgrims and the sick. In obedience to his confessor he became a priest in June 1551, at nearly thirty-six years of age.

He now began to dwell in a small community near the Church of St. Jerome, continuing his mortified life. In the same year he laid the foundation for the Congregation of the Oratory. In 1575, Gregory XIII approved it, and in 1583 gave to St. Philip the new Church of La Vallicella, which is still called La Chiesa Nuova—the New Church.

Here the Saint lived, edifying all Rome by his virtues and laboring zealously for souls in the ministry of the confessional. He enjoyed the favor of Popes Pius IV and V, Gregory XIII and XIV, and Clement VIII, and the friendship of many great men, among whom was St. Charles Borromeo.

St. Philip is said to have experienced ecstasies and visions, to have had the gift of prophecy, and to have performed miracles. Unfortunately, all of his works are lost except for a few fragments of poetry, for he burned them shortly before his death. After a life of penance and of eminent usefulness, St. Philip died in 1595, and he was canonized in 1622 by Pope Gregory XV.

PRAYER: *God, You never cease raising Your faithful servants to the glory of holiness. Grant that we may be inflamed by the fire of the Holy Spirit which so wonderfully burned in the heart of St. Philip.*

SAINT PIUS V

Pope

April 30

MICHAEL GHISLIERI was born in Italy in 1504. His whole life was always guided by the most perfect maxims of Christian piety. At age fifteen he received the Dominican habit, and at once became a model of religious perfection. In 1528, he was ordained a priest, and then taught philosophy and theology for sixteen years. He also filled other important positions in his Order.

Pope Paul IV in 1556 promoted him to the united Bishoprics of Nepi and Sutri in the Papal States, and in 1557 the same Pope created him Cardinal, but his humility and other virtues only became more conspicuous in this exalted position. Pius IV, who succeeded Paul IV in 1559, moved him to the diocese of Mondori in Piedmont. At the conclave that was held on the death of Pius IV, St. Charles Borromeo united the suffrages in favor of Cardinal Alexandrinus, as Ghislieri was called, and he became Pope under the title of Pius V in 1566.

His life as Sovereign Pontiff was as exemplary as it had been while he was a simple Dominican Friar. He immediately began putting into effect the decrees of the Council of Trent. He set up strict examinations of candidates for the priesthood and urged the founding of diocesan seminaries. At the same time, he established the Confraternity of Christian Doctrine to teach the Faith to the young.

Pius V brought simplicity to the Roman court, completed the new Catechism (1566), reformed the Breviary (1568), revised the Missal (1570), and mandated a new edition of the works of St. Thomas Aquinas, whom he proclaimed a Doctor of the Church (1567).

He sought to unite Christian monarchs against the incursions of the Turks, and it was during his pontificate that the celebrated victory of Lepanto was gained against them under Don John of Austria. As a result, he ordered the feast of the Holy Rosary to be observed on the first Sunday of October.

Pius V died in the year after this victory, on May 1, 1572, and was canonized in 1712 by Pope Clement XI.

PRAYER: *God, You raised up St. Pius to defend the Faith and achieve more suitable Divine worship. Through his intercession, help us to participate in Your mysteries with a livelier Faith and a more fruitful love.*

~ *Model of Religious Perfection* ~

~ *Patron of Travelers* ~

SAINT RAPHAEL

Archangel

September 29

NGELS are spirits without bodies, who possess superior intelligence, gigantic strength, and surpassing holiness. They enjoy an intimate relationship to God as His special adopted children, contemplating, loving, and praising Him in heaven. Some of them are frequently sent to earth as messengers from on high.

The name Raphael means "God has healed." This Angel first appears in Holy Scripture in the Book of Tobit. He acts as a guide to young Tobiah on his journey to Rages, a city in the country of the Medes, east of Nineveh, to collect a debt owed to his father. The Angel binds the demon Asmodeus in the desert of Egypt, helps Tobiah to find a wife and recover the debt, and heals Tobit from his blindness. He then reveals his identity: "I am the Angel Raphael, one of the seven who stand before the throne of God."

The Angel then goes on to say: "Bless God, and in the presence of all the living praise Him and acknowledge all the good things He has done for you. Bless and ex-tol His Name with hymns of praise. Proclaim to all people the deeds of God, and never cease to offer thanksgiving to Him.

"Prayer and fasting are worthy acts, but better than these is almsgiving with justice. A little with righteousness is better than much with wickedness. It is better to give alms than to hoard gold. For almsgiving saves us from death and purges every type of sin. Those who give alms will enjoy a long life."

Raphael is one of only three Angels (with Michael and Gabriel) identified by name in the Bible. His feast, formerly assigned to October 24, is now celebrated on September 29 together with the feasts of Sts. Michael and Gabriel.

Over the centuries, St. Raphael has been invoked by pilgrims and seamen, mountaineers and the plague-stricken, those without sight and healers—as shown by this short thousand-year-old prayer:

"Lord, send us Raphael, your messenger and bringer of graces, to show us the way and comfort us in our sorrows."

> PRAYER: *God, with great wisdom You direct the ministry of Angels and people. Grant that those who always minister to You in heaven may defend us during our life on earth.*

SAINT RITA

Religious

ST. RITA was born at Spoleto, Italy, in 1381. At an early age she begged her parents to allow her to enter a convent. Instead they arranged a marriage for her.

Rita became a good wife and mother, but her husband was a man of violent temper. In anger he often mistreated his wife. He taught their children his own evil ways. Despite his behavior, Rita tried to perform her duties faithfully and to pray and receive the Sacraments frequently.

After nearly twenty years of marriage, her husband was stabbed by an enemy. Before he died, however, he repented because Rita prayed for him.

After forgiving her husband's killers, Rita feared that her sons might exact revenge for their father's death. She prayed to God to deter them and said that she would prefer that her sons incur death rather than the serious sin of murder. As it happened both of her sons died shortly after their father.

Rita was now alone in the world, but still a loving woman. She thought of fulfilling the longings of her youth by seeking admission to the religious life. Prayers, fasting, penances of many kinds, and good works filled her days. After overcoming formidable difficulties, she was admitted to the convent of the Augustinian nuns at Cascia in Umbria and began a life of perfect obedience and great charity.

Sister Rita had a great devotion to the Passion of Christ. "Please let me suffer like You, Divine Savior," she said one day, and suddenly one of the thorns from the crucifix struck her on the forehead. It left a deep wound that did not heal and caused her much suffering for the rest of her life. She died on May 22, 1457.

St. Rita was noteworthy in that she experienced all the possible states of life and overcame the difficulties of each one with a generous love and a profound spirit of penance, while always being a peacemaker and a healer of divisions.

Rita was canonized in 1900 by Pope Leo XIII, and she has become a favorite Saint for Catholics to call upon in "impossible cases."

PRAYER: *God, through the prayers of St. Rita, may we learn to bear our crosses in life in the same spirit with which she bore hers.*

~ Patroness of Impossible Cases ~

~ *Patron of Canonists* ~

SAINT ROBERT BELLARMINE

Bishop and Doctor of the Church

September 17

BORN at Montepulciano, Italy, on October 4, 1542, St. Robert Bellarmine was the third of ten children. His mother, Cinzia Cervini, a niece of Pope Marcellus II, was dedicated to almsgiving, prayer, meditation, fasting, and mortification of the body.

Robert entered the newly formed Society of Jesus in 1560 and after his ordination went on to teach at Louvain (1570–1576), where he became famous for his Latin sermons. In 1576, the Saint was appointed to the chair of controversial theology at the Roman College, becoming Rector in 1592; he went on to become Provincial of the Naples province of the Jesuits. In 1597, he was made theologian to Clement VIII, preparing two catechisms that were used widely through modern times. He was named a Cardinal in 1599.

This outstanding scholar and devoted servant of God was in charge of preparing the Clementine revised version of the Vulgate, for which he wrote the Introduction (1592). He also defended the Apostolic See against the anti-clericals in Venice and against the political tenets of James I of England. He composed an exhaustive apologetic work against the prevailing heresies of his day. In the field of Church-state relations, he took a position based on principles now regarded as fundamentally democratic—authority originates with God, but is vested in the people, who entrust it to fit rulers.

This Saint was the spiritual father of St. Aloysius Gonzaga, helped St. Francis de Sales obtain formal approval of the Visitation Order, and in his prudence opposed severe action in the case of Galileo. It was he who is said to have advised his astronomer friend that it would be wise to advance his findings as hypotheses rather than as fully proved theories.

St. Robert has left many important writings, including works of devotion and instruction, as well as controversy. He died in 1621 and was canonized in 1930 by Pope Pius XI. The next year he was declared a Doctor of the Church by the same Pope.

PRAYER: *God, in order to vindicate Your Faith You endowed St. Robert, Your Bishop, with wondrous erudition and virtues. Through his intercession, grant that Your people may ever rejoice in the integrity of his Faith.*

SAINT ROSE OF LIMA

Virgin

August 23

ISABEL DE FLORES Y DEL OLIVA, called Rose by her mother because of her red cheeks and confirmed with that name by St. Toribio de Mogrovejo, was the first person in the Americas to be canonized as a Saint. Born in Lima, Peru, in 1586, she was often commended on her beauty and strove to hide it lest it be a source of temptation for her.

Since her parents had come upon hard economic times, Rose helped to support her family by working long hours in a garden growing flowers and then doing embroidery and other needlework well into the night. At the same time, she resisted all calls from her parents that she marry because she had taken a vow of virginity early in life.

At twenty years of age, she became a Dominican Tertiary and lived in a summer house in the garden of her home, where she became practically a recluse. Here she modeled her life after that of St. Catherine of Siena, practicing extreme penance and mortification. For example, she wore a kind of crown of thorns on her head, made of silver with little sharp prickles on the inside.

God favored her with great graces, granting her intimacy with Christ, Mary, and the Saints, who often appeared to her and confirmed her in the life she had chosen. She experienced such extraordinary mystical gifts and visions that she had to undergo an examination on the part of a commission of priests and doctors. They concluded that all of them were of supernatural origin.

St. Rose bore her many and great adversities with heroic patience and consoled the sick and suffering among the poor, Indians, and slaves. She is regarded as the originator of social service in Peru.

During the last three years of her life, sickness made it necessary for her to live in the home of Don Gonzalo de Maasa, a government official, and his wife, who was very fond of Rose. She died in 1617 at thirty-one years of age and was canonized in 1671 by Pope Clement X.

PRAYER: *God, You filled St. Rose with love for You and enabled her to give up everything and devote herself to penance. Through her intercession, help us to follow her footsteps on earth and enjoy Your blessings in heaven.*

~ *Patroness of South America* ~

~ Patron of Athletes ~

SAINT SEBASTIAN
Martyr
January 20

ST. SEBASTIAN was born at Narbonne in Gaul, educated at Milan, and martyred at Rome about the year 284.

According to an account of the fifth century and now considered unhistorical, he entered the army at Rome under the Emperor Carinus, about the year 283, in order to render assistance to the martyrs. When Diocletian left for the East, St. Sebastian continued to enjoy the esteem of Maximian, his coadjutor in the Empire.

Sebastian was instrumental in encouraging the Martyrs Marcellian and Marcus to remain steadfast in faith to the end. He also converted Nicostratus, the master of the rolls, and his wife Zoe, whom he cured of a physical affliction. He converted the jailer named Claudius, the prefect of Rome Chromatius, whom he cured of gout, and his son Tiburtius, as well as sixteen other prisoners. Most of the converts suffered martyrdom.

St. Sebastian had prudently concealed his religion, but he was at last detected and accused before Diocletian, who condemned him to be shot to death by arrow. The sentence was executed to the extent that he was left for dead.

Irene, the widow of St. Castulus, went to bury him and found him still alive. She brought him to her lodgings and restored him to health. However, St. Sebastian refused to flee. Instead, he boldly appeared before Diocletian and reproached him for his injustice against the Christians.

Diocletian was astonished to see Sebastian alive, but he quickly recovered from his surprise and commanded that he be beaten to death with clubs and his body thrown into the common sewer. A pious woman learned of its whereabouts and had it removed and buried in the catacombs.

The Church stresses that the main facts about Sebastian are true. He was a Roman martyr, but most likely connected with Milan also, since he was venerated there from ancient times. He was buried on the Appian Way, probably near the basilica later built in his name. Devotion to him was widespread in the Middle Ages, and he was customarily pictured as a young man pierced with arrows.

PRAYER: *Lord, grant us a spirit of strength. Taught by the glorious example of Your Martyr St. Sebastian, may we learn how to obey You rather than other human beings.*

SAINT STEPHEN

First Martyr

December 26

ST. STEPHEN, a disciple of Christ, chosen after the Ascension as one of the seven deacons, and "full of grace and fortitude, was working great wonders and signs among the people." Many rose up against him, but they were not able to withstand the wisdom with which he spoke so fearlessly.

Therefore, Stephen was denounced to the Sanhedrin for blasphemy against God and against Moses because he had foretold the end of the Mosaic dispensation and the destruction of the Temple. Stephen's reply to these charges constitutes the longest speech in the Acts of the Apostles.

He summarizes the history of the chosen people during the periods of the Patriarchs, Moses, David, and Solomon, solemnly professing his belief in God and his reverence for the Law and the Temple. He sets forth the following points. Abraham was justified and received God's favors in a foreign land. Solomon built the Temple, but God could not be confined in houses made by hands. The Temple and the Mosaic Law were to stand only until God introduced more excellent institutions by sending the Messiah Himself.

So convincing was Stephen's speech that when he denounced the stubborn resistance put up by the people and exclaimed, "Look, I see the heavens opened, and the Son of Man standing at God's right hand," his hearers could take no more. They dragged him outside the city gates and stoned him while he was invoking Jesus ("Lord Jesus, receive my spirit") and praying for his slayers ("Lord, do not hold this sin against them"). And when he had said this, he fell asleep in the Lord in the year 35 A.D.

It is believed that by his martyrdom Stephen won the grace of conversion for Saul, who was guarding the coats of those who carried out the death sentence.

In the fifth century, Stephen's remains were placed in the basilica built by the Empress Eudoxia in 460 on the site of his death.

PRAYER: *God, grant that we may imitate the Saint we honor and learn to love our enemies. For every December we celebrate the feast of St. Stephen who knew how to pray even for his persecutors.*

~ *Patron of Stonemasons* ~

~ *Patroness of Headache-Sufferers* ~

SAINT TERESA OF AVILA

Virgin and Doctor of the Church

October 15

ST. TERESA was born on March 28, 1515, in Avila, Spain. Her mother died when she was twelve and her father placed her in a convent of Augustinian nuns. When she returned home, she determined to enter religious life. She became a nun in the Carmelite Convent of the Incarnation, near Avila, and made her profession in November 1534.

Though for many years in the convent she led a good religious life, certain faults still adhered to her; but the moment of grace came at last and the noble heart of St. Teresa began to soar upward to perfection. Inspired by the Holy Spirit and acting under the direction of enlightened men, among whom was St. Peter of Alcantara, she undertook the superhuman task of reforming her Order and restoring its primitive observance.

Assisted by St. John of the Cross, she succeeded in establishing the Reform of the Discalced Carmelites, for both the brethren and the sisters of her Order. Before her death in 1582, thirty-two monasteries of the Reformed Rule had been established, among which seventeen were convents of nuns. She was canonized in 1622 by Pope Gregory XV.

St. Teresa wrote letters and books that are classics of spiritual literature. Among them are her *Autobiography* (written at the request of her directors), *The Way of Perfection* (intended for the guidance of her nuns), *The Book of Foundations* (intended for the edification and encouragement of her nuns), and *The Interior Castle* (written for the instruction of the Church).

St. Teresa received great gifts from God in the supernatural order as well as in the natural order. She had splendid natural talents, such as sweetness of temperament, affectionate tenderness of heart, lively wit and imagination, and deep psychological insight. And all her gifts combined to set forth her writings on Mystical Theology, which Popes Gregory XV and Urban VII considered to be equal to those of a Doctor of the Church. Hence, on September 27, 1970, Pope Paul VI added her name to the roll of the Doctors of the Church.

PRAYER: *God, You raised up St. Teresa by Your Spirit so that she could manifest to the Church the way to perfection. Nourish us with the food of heaven, and fire us with a desire for holiness.*

SAINT THERESE OF THE CHILD JESUS

Virgin and Doctor of the Church

October 1

BORN at Alençon in Normandy, France, in 1873, Marie Frances Therese Martin entered the Carmel of Lisieux in 1889, at age fifteen, and on September 30, 1897, she winged her flight to heaven. She was canonized in 1925 by Pope Pius XI (only 28 years after her death) and was named the third woman Doctor of the Church by Pope John Paul II on October 19, 1997.

The story of those nine years is faithfully told in her *Autobiography,* which the Little Flower, as she came to be known, wrote under obedience. Every line is marked by the artless simplicity of a literary genius, so that even when translated from its musical euphonious French into English, it still reads with the rhythm of a prose poem.

She took for her motto the well-known words of the great Carmelite mystic St. John of the Cross: "Love is repaid by love alone." With these thoughts ever present in her mind, her heart found courage to endure hours and days of bitterness that few Saints have been privileged to undergo. She understood deeply the meaning of those mysterious words of St. Paul: "Far be it from me to glory save in the Cross of my Lord Jesus Christ, by which I am crucified to the world and the world is crucified to me. I fill up those things that are wanting in the sufferings of Christ for His members."

Love of God as a Father, expressed in childlike simplicity and trust, and a deep understanding of the mystery of the Cross were the basic principles of Therese's "little way."

There is just one other doctrine that needs to be mentioned to complete the picture of her soul's surrender—her vivid realization of the spiritual Motherhood of Mary, the Mother of God, and heaven's Queen, and our own loving Mother. She had learned the meaning of the strong phrase of St. Augustine, written fifteen hundred years ago, that we were all begotten with Jesus in the womb of Mary as our Mother.

PRAYER: *God our Father, You destined Your Kingdom for Your children who are humble. Help us to imitate the way of St. Therese, so that, by her intercession, we may attain the eternal glory that You promised.*

~ Patroness of the Missions ~

~ Patron of Architects ~

SAINT THOMAS

Apostle

July 3

ST. THOMAS was a Jew, called to be one of the twelve Apostles. He was a dedicated but impetuous follower of Christ. When Jesus said that He was returning to Judea to visit His sick friend Lazarus, Thomas immediately exhorted the other Apostles to accompany Him on the trip, which involved certain danger and possible death because of the mounting hostility of the authorities. At the Last Supper, when Christ told His Apostles that He was going to prepare a place for them to which they also might come because they knew both the place and the way, Thomas pleaded that they did not understand and received the beautiful assurance that Christ is the Way, the Truth, and the Life.

But St. Thomas is best known for his role in verifying the Resurrection of His Master. Thomas's unwillingness to believe that the other Apostles had seen their Risen Lord on the first Easter Sunday merited for him the title of "doubting Thomas." Eight days later, on Christ's second apparition, Thomas was gently rebuked for his skepticism and furnished with the evidence he had demanded—seeing in Christ's hands the point of the nails and putting his fingers in the place of the nails and his hand into His side. At this, St. Thomas became convinced of the truth of the Resurrection and exclaimed: "My Lord and my God," thus making a public Profession of Faith in the Divinity of Jesus.

St. Thomas is also mentioned as being present at another Resurrection appearance of Jesus—at Lake Tiberias when a miraculous catch of fish occurred. This is all that we know about St. Thomas from the New Testament.

Tradition says that at the dispersal of the Apostles after Pentecost this Saint was sent to evangelize the Parthians, Medes, and Persians; he ultimately reached India, carrying the Faith to the Malabar coast, which still boasts a large native population calling themselves "Christians of St. Thomas." This Apostle capped his life by shedding his blood for His Master, speared to death at a place called Calamine.

PRAYER: *Almighty God, may we be helped by the patronage of St. Thomas the Apostle and, believing, have life in the Name of Jesus Christ Your Son Whom he confessed to be the Lord.*

SAINT THOMAS AQUINAS

Priest and Doctor of the Church

January 28

ST. THOMAS, born toward the end of 1226, was the son of Landulph, Count of Aquino, who, when St. Thomas was five years old, placed him under the care of the Benedictines of Monte Cassino. His progress surprised his teachers, for he surpassed all his fellow pupils in learning as well as in the practice of virtue.

When he became of age to choose his state of life, St. Thomas renounced the things of this world and resolved to enter the Order of St. Dominic in spite of the opposition of his family. In 1243, at the age of seventeen, he joined the Dominicans of Naples. All efforts of family members to dissuade him from his vocation failed, and St. Thomas persevered. As a reward for his fidelity, God conferred upon him the gift of perfect chastity, which has merited for him the title of the Angelic Doctor.

After making his profession at Naples, he studied at Cologne under the celebrated St. Albert the Great. Here he was nicknamed the "Dumb Ox" because of his silent ways and huge size, but he was really a brilliant student. At twenty-two, he was appointed to teach in the same city. At that time he also began to publish his first works. After four years he was sent to Paris. The Saint, then a priest, received his doctorate at the age of thirty-one.

In 1261 Urban IV called him to Rome, where he was appointed to teach, but he positively declined to accept any ecclesiastical dignity. St. Thomas not only wrote (his writings fill twenty hefty tomes characterized by brilliance of thought and lucidity of language), but he preached often and with the greatest fruit. Clement IV offered him the Archbishopric of Naples, which he also refused.

He left the great monument of his learning, the *Summa Theologica*, unfinished, for on his way to the Second Council of Lyons, ordered there by Gregory X, he fell sick, and died at the Cistercian monastery of Fossa Nuova in 1274. He was canonized in 1323 by Pope John XXII.

PRAYER: *Father of wisdom, You inspired St. Thomas Aquinas with an ardent desire for holiness and study of sacred doctrine. Help us, we pray, to understand what he taught and to imitate what he lived.*

~ *Patron of Schools* ~

~ Patron of Lawyers ~

SAINT THOMAS MORE

Martyr

June 22

ST. THOMAS MORE was born at London in 1478. After a thorough grounding in religion and the classics, he entered Oxford to study law. Then he embarked on a legal career that took him to Parliament. In 1505, he married his beloved Jane Colt who bore him four children, and when she died at a young age he married a widow, Alice Middleton, to be a mother for his young children.

Thomas's house in Chelsea became a center of intellectual life, which graced the presence of such figures as the leading Renaissance thinker Erasmus. Thomas himself became one of the leading lights of his time, honored for his intellect and scholarship. He composed poetry, history, treatises, devotional literature, and Latin translations.

A wit and a reformer, this learned man numbered Bishops and scholars among his friends, and by 1516 wrote his world-famous book *Utopia*. It describes an ideal community living according to the natural law and practicing a natural religion, with satiric barbs thrown in at abuses current in his day.

Henry VIII appointed him to a succession of high posts, and finally Lord Chancellor in 1529. However, he resigned in 1532, at the height of his career, when Henry persisted in holding his own opinions regarding marriage and the supremacy of the Pope.

The rest of his life was spent in writing, mostly in defense of the Church. In 1534, with his close friend, St. John Fisher, he refused to render allegiance to the King as the Head of the Church of England and was confined to the Tower. Fifteen months later, and nine days after St. John Fisher's execution, he was convicted of treason.

St. Thomas told the court that he could not go against his conscience and wished his judges that "we may yet hereafter in heaven merrily all meet together to everlasting salvation." And on the scaffold he told the crowd of spectators that he was dying as "the King's good servant—but God's first." He was beheaded on July 6, 1535, and canonized in 1935 by Pope Pius XI.

> PRAYER: *God, You consummated the form of the true Faith in martyrdom. Through the intercession of St. Thomas, grant that we may confirm by the testimony of our lives the Faith we profess with our tongues.*

SAINT VINCENT DE PAUL

Priest

September 27

ST. VINCENT was born of poor parents in the village of Pouy in Gascony, France, about 1580. He enjoyed his first schooling under the Franciscan Fathers at Acqs. Such had been his progress in four years that a gentleman chose him as a tutor for his children, and he was thus enabled to continue his studies without being a burden to his parents. In 1596, he went to the University of Toulouse for theological studies, and there he was ordained a priest in 1600.

In 1605, on a voyage by sea from Marseilles to Narbonne, he fell into the hands of African pirates and was carried as a slave to Tunis. His captivity lasted about two years, until Divine Providence enabled him to effect his escape. After a brief visit to Rome he returned to France, where he became tutor in the family of Emmanuel de Gondy, Count of Joigny, and general of the galleys of France.

In 1617, Vincent began to preach missions, and in 1625 he laid the foundations of a congregation that afterward became the Congregation of the Mission, or Lazarists, so named on account of the Priory of St. Lazarus, which the Fathers began to occupy in 1633.

It would be impossible to enumerate all the works of this servant of God. Charity was his predominant virtue. It extended to all classes of persons, from forsaken childhood to old age. The Sisters of Charity also owe the foundation of their congregation to St. Vincent.

In the midst of the most distracting occupations the Saint's soul was always intimately united with God. Though honored by the great ones of the world, he remained deeply rooted in humility. The Apostle of Charity, the immortal Vincent de Paul, breathed his last in Paris at the age of eighty, September 27, 1660. He was canonized in 1737 by Pope Clement XII.

PRAYER: *God, You gave St. Vincent de Paul apostolic virtues for the salvation of the poor and the formation of the clergy. Grant that, endowed with the same spirit, we may love what he loved and act according to his teaching.*

~ Patron of Charitable Societies ~

PRAYER TO A
PATRON SAINT

DEAR Saint,
I am honored to bear your name—
a name made famous by your heroic virtues.
Help me never to do anything to besmirch it.
Obtain God's grace for me
that I may grow in faith, hope, and love,
and all the virtues.
Grant that by imitating you
I may imitate our Lord and Master, Jesus Christ.
Watch over me along the way of the rest of my life
and bring me safe to my heavenly home at my death.

OTHER OUTSTANDING CATHOLIC BOOKS

HOLY BIBLE—Saint Joseph Edition of the completely modern translation called the New American Bible. Printed in large type with helpful Notes and Maps, Photographs, Family Record Pages, and Bible Dictionary.

Family Edition	**No. 612**
Full Size Edition	**No. 611**
Medium Size Edition	**No. 609**
Giant Type Edition	**No. 616**
Personal Size Edition	**No. 510**

BIBLE MEDITATIONS FOR EVERY DAY—By Rev. John Kersten, S.V.D. Excellent aid for daily meditation on the Word of God. A scripture passage and a short invaluable introduction are given for every day of the year. The author deals with themes relevant to today's living and thus brings the Faith home to his readers. **No. 277**

NEW TESTAMENT—St. Joseph Edition of the New Catholic Version. Large, easy-to-read type, with helpful Notes and Maps, Photographs, and Study Guide. Features words of Christ in red.

Study Edition	**No. 311**
Vest Pocket Edition—legible type. Illustrated.	**No. 650**

PICTURE BOOK OF SAINTS—By Rev. Lawrence G. Lovasik, S.V.D. Illustrated lives of the Saints in full color for young and old. It clearly depicts the lives of over 100 popular Saints in word and picture, including 16 modern-day Saints. **No. 235**

MY FIRST PRAYERBOOK—By Rev. Lawrence G. Lovasik, S.V.D. Beautiful prayerbook that provides prayers for the main occasions in a child's life. Features simple language, easy-to-read type, and full-color illustrations. **No. 205**

THE MASS FOR CHILDREN—By Rev. Jude Winkler, OFM Conv. Beautifully illustrated Mass Book that explains the Mass to children and contains the Mass responses they should know. It is sure to help children know and love the Mass. **No. 215**

NEW CATHOLIC PICTURE BIBLE—By Rev. Lawrence G. Lovasik, S.V.D. Stories taken from the Holy Bible, intended for the whole family and easy to understand. **No. 435**

GREAT PEOPLE OF THE BIBLE—By Rev. Jude Winkler, OFM Conv. Full-page portrait of more than 70 biblical personages accompanied by a concise one-page biography. **No. 485**